Bread and wine people

An all-age on-going parish training programme for full participation in the Eucharist

SUSAN SAYERS

Illustrated by Arthur Baker
and Fred Chevalier

Kevin Mayhew

First published in 2001 by
KEVIN MAYHEW LTD
Buxhall, Stowmarket
Suffolk IP14 3BW

9 8 7 6 5 4 3 2 1 0

ISBN 1 84003 694 X
Catalogue No. 1500411

Cover design by Jonathan Stroulger
Edited by Katherine Laidler
Typesetting by Richard Weaver

Printed in Great Britain

Contents

Introduction

Required reading!

Week by week all over the world the Christian community gathers to worship God and share in Communion. Increasingly parishes are wanting to include their committed, baptised children in this regular feeding, and there is widespread recognition that some kind of training is an essential part of this.

Naturally no one wants the entire spiritual nurture of the Christian family to be reduced simply to a short course of lessons after which the young children 'graduate' to receive Communion at the Eucharist along with the adults. Neither are existing Confirmation courses suitable, either in age level or content.

It seems sensible to use this as a wonderful opportunity to think seriously about how any of us are deepening our faith, whatever our age, and whether, rather than a one-off course, we should be looking at ensuring that our parishes are providing on-going spiritual nurture for all ages. Baptised children could then come naturally to receive Communion at whatever age was considered suitable, since they would already be part of the on-going parish programme.

The great advantage of this approach is that it proclaims our belief in all being part of the Community of Faith. It celebrates the reality that we are a travelling people, all learning and benefiting from one another, and all supporting and encouraging one another. Supremely the Eucharist focuses on our feeding as the Body of Christ, and surely the best way of passing this on to any new members, of whatever age, is to explore its riches communally and in the context of the Eucharist.

Accordingly I have tried to make this on-going course a shared journey of discovery for the whole Community of Faith. For each of the three years of the Common Worship Lectionary there are four parish teaching Eucharists and one shared teaching meal. The three yearly meals are a Passover celebration, a fellowship meal, and an Emmaus meal. The teaching Eucharists are spread throughout the year and are designed to help deepen a sense of community in the parish, so I suggest that the worship on these days concludes with a shared lunch or picnic. Then, in the context of real community, Christians of all ages can learn together what it means to be the Body of Christ. We could call it a multi-sensory or holistic learning experience, but in reality it is simply taking seriously our calling to be a loving, serving community, with Jesus present among us.

How does it all work?

THE TEACHING EUCHARISTS

Four times each year the lectionary readings are explored in the Eucharist by all age groups, with a special focus on what it means to be a Eucharistic community. This means that over three years the whole community will have covered twelve different areas of faith development. Each section can be easily adapted as required. If preferred, the material could be used on four parish days during the year – on Saturdays or during the week, or on a parish holiday as the main focus of the teaching programme.

Many parishes are already familiar with the *Living Stones* programme, so the format is linked with that. There are Pebbles, Rocks and Boulders sections for children and young people, and there is a suggested focus for adults as well. The difference is that at these teaching Eucharists the whole community begins and rounds off the liturgy of the word with a shared activity in church which picks up on what everyone is doing in their separate age groups. Everyone will find they need the input of the other age groups and all will be directly learning from one another. The all-age ideas for the worship are designed to fit in with this format, and a simple commentary is suggested so that the whole service is a learning experience as well as a time of worship and Communion.

Probably the service will be a little longer than usual, but with all age groups actively involved this should not be a problem, so long as everyone knows well in advance and is involved in the preparation so that everyone 'owns' it. Follow the service with some shared fellowship, either by going for a walk and a picnic, or sharing a 'pot luck' lunch together.

Careful, organised preparation is essential for each teaching Eucharist. This is all part of the worship and the training, since people will have to communicate and work together. Here is a suggested plan to follow:

- **Well in advance** make known the dates for the next year's four teaching Eucharists.
- **A month beforehand** meet with the leaders of children, young people and adults, and whoever is giving the all-age talk. Pray together, look at the main focus of learning, copy relevant material and give everyone an order of service. Check that everyone knows their area of responsibility in preparation and in the service.
- **A week beforehand** check that all preparations are complete.
- **Half an hour beforehand** check that the different areas of the church are prepared, and pray together.

THE ANNUAL MEAL

In addition to these training Eucharists, once a year the course teaches through a shared parish celebration meal, which can become an annual tradition. Three basic frameworks are provided, with activities, food, sketches, copiable and age-related placemats and so on, to take the stress out of the planning and practicalities. The material is flexible and adaptable.

The Rocks and Pebbles material for this whole course is designed to build into a book, in order to be a useful form of reference for the children and a refresher course to work through just before they receive Communion for the first time. It is recommended that the children will have completed at least one full year of the material before this.

The adults and young people are also provided with handouts to keep in a folder, with suggestions for further thinking and reading. This can be used individually and in small group work if required. It can also form the bulk of confirmation preparation.

Section One
TEACHING EUCHARISTS

YEAR A

Second Sunday of Advent – Year A

Repentance

Thought for the day

Let's make a clear road to get ourselves ready for welcoming Jesus.

Reflection on the readings

Isaiah 11:1-10
Psalm 72:1-7, 18-19
Romans 15:4-13
Matthew 3:1-12

Today Paul reminds us of the teaching and encouragement we are given through the scriptures, so that we maintain our hope. By the end of the passage he's talking about us overflowing with hope, once we've got into the habit of being constantly topped up by God, who is, after all, the ground of all hope. And with the hope come all kinds of other good things, like joy and peace and a life of faith in the Spirit's power.

Hope is linked with longing: longing for all the good things we sense life was meant to be like, but which it so often falls short of. 'One day . . . ,' the prophet dreams in our first reading from Isaiah; one day it will be as we all long for it to be, with righteousness and real justice, and no conflict or cruelty.

Is it just a dream? Almost like an alarm clock, John the Baptist bursts into our longings and starts shaking us into action. It is the action of thorough, deep-seated repentance, so that we may be prepared and ready for Jesus to save us and make the dream kingdom a practical reality. So that we are ready to come when he says follow; so that we actually notice him calling us.

Every time we come to the Eucharist we need to prepare ourselves to meet with Jesus, which is why we start off the service with a time of Confession. How can we best use this provision? Clearly real repentance is far less likely to happen if we just read through the words on a Sunday without thinking much about them. The truth is that every time we realise we are thinking, acting or speaking unlovingly, bitterly, destructively, dishonestly or unfairly, we need to repent immediately and make ourselves right with God, whose love and truth our living has insulted. Then, when we gather as the community of faith at the Eucharist, bringing to mind all those times from the last week, we shall be making a communal act of real repentance, and clearing the road for Jesus to come to us and make his home with us.

Discussion starters

1. Why do we need to repent and confess our sins when we gather to worship God and receive Communion?
2. Read through the words of the General Confessions on the worksheet on page 21, looking at what they suggest we should be sorting out in our lives. Have we become calloused to any of these, so we no longer count them as needing repentance?
3. As the church community here, what things do we perhaps need to repent of together? Are there any long-standing blocks (such as wrong attitudes, misplaced priorities) on the road which we've stopped noticing because we are so accustomed to them? Get rid of them now by repenting together of them, and resolving to address them.

Suggested order of service

Things to do and people to do them

The people and the priest:

greet each other in the Lord's name
(included in the welcome is an introduction to this teaching Eucharist, and the logistics of it – just for today, the time of Confession will take place later on in the service, as it follows on from what everyone is doing in their groups)

keep silence and pray a Collect

proclaim and respond to the Word of God
- Isaiah 11:1-10 – this is read as a community
- Romans 15:4-13 – choose an appropriate version such as *The Message* by Eugene Peterson
- Matthew 3:1-12 – the Gospel is being dramatised by the children
- After the Gospel, Pebbles, Rocks, Boulders and adults respond to the Word in their own teaching, in different parts of the church
- All-age talk gathers these responses together

confess their sins and are assured of God's forgiveness
(led by the adults, this grows out of the response to the Word of God)

pray for the Church and the world
(the Intercessions today are being organised and led by the Boulders)

exchange the Peace

prepare the table
(a hymn is sung and the gifts of bread and wine are brought by representatives; offerings of money are also collected and dedicated to God's service)

pray the Eucharistic Prayer
(the children can gather around the altar; older children and young people can hold lighted candles)

receive Communion
(hymns and songs can be sung as everyone gathers to receive God's gifts)

depart with God's blessing

Communal reading of Isaiah 11:1-10

All	**A shoot will come up from the stump of Jesse: from his roots a Branch will bear fruit.**
Children	The Spirit of the Lord will rest on him –
Women/girls	the Spirit of wisdom and of understanding,
Men/boys	the Spirit of counsel and of power,
Women/girls	the Spirit of knowledge and of the fear of the Lord –
Men/boys	and he will delight in the fear of the Lord.
All	**He will not judge by what he sees with his eyes, or decide by what he hears with his ears;**
Men/boys	but with righteousness he will judge the needy,
Women/girls	with justice he will give decisions for the poor of the earth.
Men/boys	He will strike the earth with the rod of his mouth;
Women/girls	with the breath of his lips he will slay the wicked.
All	**Righteousness will be his belt and faithfulness the sash round his waist.**
Men/boys	The wolf will live with the lamb, the leopard will lie down with the goat,
All	**the calf and the lion and the yearling together;**
Children	and a little child will lead them.
Women/girls	The cow will feed with the bear, their young will lie down together,
Children	and the lion will eat straw like the ox.
Men/boys	The infant will play near the hole of the cobra,
Women/girls	and the young child put his hand into the viper's nest.
All	**They will neither harm nor destroy on all my holy mountain, for the earth will be full of the knowledge of the Lord as the waters cover the sea.**

All-age exploration of the Word
PEBBLES

Second Sunday of Advent – Year A

Repentance

Thought for the day

Let's make a clear road to get ourselves ready for welcoming Jesus.

Readings

Isaiah 11:1-10
Psalm 72:1-7, 18-19
Romans 15:4-13
Matthew 3:1-12

Before the service (advance preparation)

- Prepare a long roll of wallpaper or lining paper by sticking on to it lots of pictures copied and cut from the worksheet. You will need lots of each picture. Have this fixed to the floor of the church, along the central aisle.
- Copy the worksheets and provide plenty of crayons. Have the children's folders ready.
- Arrange an area of the church where you will gather for the teaching.

During the service

- After the Gospel, gather the children together.

Teaching

Give out the worksheets. On them is an example of each picture you have stuck on the roll of lining paper. Look at these pictures, naming them as you go.

Talk with the children about what kind of things we say and do when we are being unkind, unfair, cruel, and so on, and how all these things make God sad. They are like big rocks in the middle of the road which stop God from being with us. But when we are sorry about them and ask God to forgive us, it's like pushing all those rocks out of the way so there is a good clear road for God to come to us, and for us to run to meet him.

Now talk about the sort of things we think and say and do which make God happy, like helping one another, being kind and thoughtful, enjoying life and helping others enjoy it as well. All these things are like building a good strong, beautiful road for God to walk to us and us to run to meet him.

Take the children to the long 'road' which we are making to help all the other people in church know about getting ourselves ready for Jesus. They are going to scribble out all the things we want to get rid of in our lives and which make God sad, and colour in all the loving things which make God happy

All together

During the All-age Talk the children can walk up and down their road, pointing out the things which we need to get rid of because they are unloving and make God sad, and then all the loving things which make God happy.

Notes

we turn back to Jesus
Being unfair
Being cruel and unkind
hee hee!
Fighting
Being selfish
Helping one another
Enjoying God's world
Being generous
we say:
I'm sorry!

All-age exploration of the Word
ROCKS

Second Sunday of Advent – Year A

Repentance

Thought for the day

Let's make a clear road to get ourselves ready for welcoming Jesus.

Readings

Isaiah 11:1-10
Psalm 72:1-7, 18-19
Romans 15:4-13
Matthew 3:1-12

Before the service (advance preparation)

- Copy the worksheets and arrange a place in the church for the teaching, preferably next to the font. You will need a flipchart or large sheet, a marker pen, blutack, and coloured pencils. Have a jug of water in the font.
- Have the children's folders ready.
- Prepare the Gospel as a dramatised reading, with John the Baptist dressed up and walking slowly down the aisle from the back shouting his message. Others of the group (dressed up, if possible) come out from all over the church and mime being baptised in the Jordan. The rest of the group are the Pharisees and Sadducees coming for baptism. The narrator reads the text, and you could have adults (hidden and using another microphone) who read the voice-over for John the Baptist.
- Prepare cards with opposite words on either side: Selfishness/Love, Evil/Good, and Wrong/Right.

During the service

- The group act out their dramatised reading of the Gospel. After this, gather them to the area near the font.

Teaching
What happens here? Pour some water into the font and see how many things they can come up with that water does (such as washing, cooking, quenching thirst, drowning, holding you up, sustaining life, growing, recycling, and so on). Water does all this, so it's a really good sign for new life. When we are baptised we are dipped in water as a sign that we have drowned to the old ways of selfishness and sin, and are being born again as a child of our loving God. (Have a brief 'any questions' slot at this point.)

Can anyone remember what John the Baptist was telling everyone to do just before he baptised them? He was telling them to *repent*. (Write the word large on a flipchart.) To re-pent means to turn round and face the other way. (They can try this, and you can write it next to 'Repent'.) John was saying to them, 'Look how your lives are facing the wrong way – turn yourselves around and face God's way, so you're ready for when he comes to you!' Then, as a sign that their wrong thinking and behaviour was being washed away, he baptised them, dipping them under the water in the River Jordan. When they came up out of the water, they were all ready to start living with their lives facing in God's direction.

Whenever we come to worship, we start by telling God we are sorry for facing the wrong way – facing selfishness instead of love, wrong instead of right, evil instead of good. (Stick up these words on the chart as you say them, bad side to the front.) When we *repent*, or turn right round to face the other way, we will be turning from selfishness to love, from wrong to right, and from evil to good. (Different children can turn the cards round as each is mentioned.)

Using their worksheets, the children reinforce the teaching on repentance.

All together
The children show everyone else what the word 'Repent' means, by physically turning to face the opposite direction. Three of them can then hold and turn the cards, while the others shout out, 'Turn from selfishness to love; turn from wrong to right; turn from evil to good!'

Notes

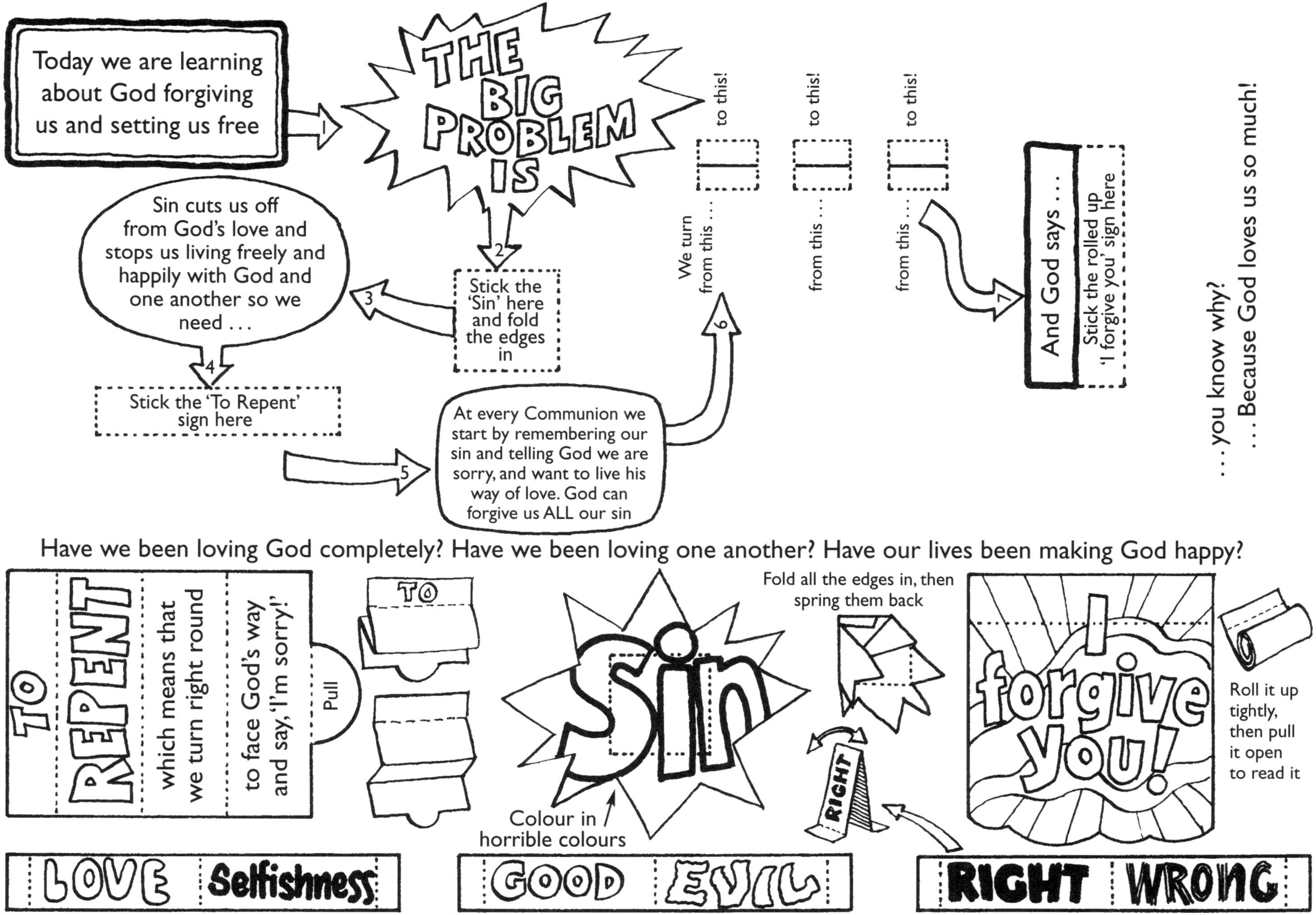
Today we are learning about God forgiving us and setting us free
1
THE BIG PROBLEM IS
2
Stick the 'Sin' here and fold the edges in
3
Sin cuts us off from God's love and stops us living freely and happily with God and one another so we need . . .
4
Stick the 'To Repent' sign here
5
At every Communion we start by remembering our sin and telling God we are sorry, and want to live his way of love. God can forgive us ALL our sin
6
We turn from this . . .
to this!
from this . . .
to this!
from this . . .
to this!
7
And God says . . .
Stick the rolled up 'I forgive you' sign here
. . . you know why?
. . . Because God loves us so much!
Have we been loving God completely? Have we been loving one another? Have our lives been making God happy?
TO
REPENT
which means that we turn right round
to face God's way and say, 'I'm sorry!'
Pull
TO
Sin
Colour in horrible colours
Fold all the edges in, then spring them back
RIGHT
I forgive you!
Roll it up tightly, then pull it open to read it
LOVE
Selfishness
GOOD
EVIL
RIGHT
WRONG

All-age exploration of the Word
BOULDERS

Second Sunday of Advent – Year A

Repentance

Thought for the day

Let's make a clear road to get ourselves ready for welcoming Jesus.

Readings

Isaiah 11:1-10
Psalm 72:1-7, 18-19
Romans 15:4-13
Matthew 3:1-12

Before the service (advance preparation)

- Prepare this week's Intercessions, with four collages of images and words mounted on A1 paper (flipchart size) and displayed around the church. Collage 1 has images of the church and local area, local schools and shops, and church leaders; collage 2 has national and international causes for concern; collage 3 has ordinary, everyday images of homes and families, friends and neighbours; and collage 4 has images associated with those who are unwell, imprisoned, frail and sad. Each collage has on it 'Lord, hear our prayer'. Suitable music, to help people pray, is chosen and played while people are invited to make their way quietly around the church, praying as they look at the images. Young children can go round with an adult or older child who can help them pray as well.
- Arrange an area for the teaching, have their folders ready and copy the worksheets.

During the service

- After the Gospel, gather the group together.

Teaching
Try the quiz on the sheet, for which Bibles will be needed. There is also a short script for two of them to read as a discussion starter.

All together
The 'Turn your life around' script will be part of the all-age talk. Arrange for everyone to shout the title, and two people to speak the conversation, slowly and using the sound system.

- After the Creed, the Boulders introduce the Intercessions, and when everyone has visited each prayer site, they gather all the prayers up, saying:

Merciful Father,
accept these prayers
for the sake of your Son
our Saviour Jesus Christ. Amen.

Notes

TURN YOUR LIFE AROUND

WHY IS THERE A PRAYER OF CONFESSION AT THE BEGINNING OF WORSHIP?

Well, we're all gathering together to meet with God and worship him, but we all know we haven't been the loving church of people we're called to be.

SO YOU MEAN WE'RE PUTTING OURSELVES RIGHT WITH GOD BEFORE WE HAVE THE NERVE TO WORSHIP HIM?

Exactly. How can we realistically offer worship to the loving God when we haven't apologised for all the unloving stuff we've done, and the loving we haven't bothered to do?

WHAT'S IT CALLED AGAIN – THIS TURNING AWAY FROM SIN TOWARDS GOD?

Repentance. We repent of our sin, and God forgives us, which sets us free of it for ever.

1. **Why is God refusing to listen to the people's prayers?**
   (a) Their lives show they don't mean what they're saying
   (b) They aren't dressed properly
   (c) They aren't speaking loud enough
2. **What does God tell the people to do?**
   (a) Pray with more words
   (b) Stop doing evil and learn to do good
   (c) Stop coming to worship

1. **When John urged people to repent, what did they do?**
   (a) They decided he couldn't mean them as they hadn't sinned
   (b) They kept quiet about their sins as they were embarrassed
   (c) They publicly confessed their sins and John washed them clean in baptism
2. **How were people told their repentance would be proved true?**
   (a) By going through the water
   (b) By the good fruit their lives would produce
   (c) By pretending they were sorry

1. **What will God do, as we lead the life of faith?**
   (a) Send us on a guilt trip
   (b) Make us into sad freaks
   (c) Fill us all with joy and peace, until, by the power of the Holy Spirit, we overflow with hope

All-age exploration of the Word
ADULTS

Second Sunday of Advent – Year A

Repentance

Thought for the day

Let's make a clear road to get ourselves ready for welcoming Jesus.

Readings

Isaiah 11:1-10
Psalm 72:1-7, 18-19
Romans 15:4-13
Matthew 3:1-12

Before the service (advance preparation)

- Arrange for some small-group leaders to lead discussion in groups all over the church. Each leader will need enough sheets for their group, a bible and a bowl of water.
- Have the Isaiah passage copied for a communal reading.

During the service

- The passage from Isaiah is read communally. This is given on page 13 with sections to be read by the men and boys, women and girls, everyone together and the children only, as indicated.
- After the Gospel, the adults move into small groups, with a leader.

Teaching
On the sheet are the Bible references for today, and the reflection on the readings, several examples of General Confessions, and three discussion starters. There is also space to record any notes on the discussion or reading.

All together
During the All-age Talk representatives from the groups will be invited to share what they discovered was valuable about confessing our sins together at the start of the Communion service.

- Some of the adults lead everyone in a time of confession, which takes place today straight after the plenary session. Standing with their backs to the cross, everyone is invited to bring to mind things in their attitudes, thoughts, words or behaviour in which they are turning their back on God's way of love and truth. This is done in silence. Then everyone turns right round to face the cross, confessing their sins together, using the words of one of the Confessions from the adult worksheet, which will have been printed on the service sheet, and the priest or minister pronounces God's forgiveness.

Notes

Repentance

Thought for the day

Let's make a clear road to get ourselves ready for welcoming Jesus.

Reflection on the readings

Isaiah 11:1-10
Psalm 72:1-7, 18-19
Romans 15:4-13
Matthew 3:1-12

Today Paul reminds us of the teaching and encouragement we are given through the scriptures, so that we maintain our hope. By the end of the passage he's talking about us overflowing with hope, once we've got into the habit of being constantly topped up by God, who is, after all, the ground of all hope. And with the hope come all kinds of other good things, like joy and peace and a life of faith in the Spirit's power.

Hope is linked with longing: longing for all the good things we sense life was meant to be like, but which it so often falls short of. 'One day . . . ,' the prophet dreams in our first reading from Isaiah; one day it will be as we all long for it to be, with righteousness and real justice, and no conflict or cruelty.

Is it just a dream? Almost like an alarm clock, John the Baptist bursts into our longings and starts shaking us into action. It is the action of thorough, deep-seated repentance, so that we may be prepared and ready for Jesus to save us and make the dream kingdom a practical reality. So that we are ready to come when he says follow; so that we actually notice him calling us.

Every time we come to the Eucharist we need to prepare ourselves to meet with Jesus, which is why we start off the service with a time of confession. How can we best use this provision? Clearly real repentance is far less likely to happen if we just read through the words on a Sunday without thinking much about them. The truth is that every time we realise we are thinking, acting or speaking unlovingly, bitterly, destructively, dishonestly or unfairly, we need to repent immediately and make ourselves right with God, whose love and truth our living has insulted. Then, when we gather as the community of faith at the Eucharist, bringing to mind all those times from the last week, we shall be making a communal act of real repentance, and clearing the road for Jesus to come to us and make his home with us.

Discussion starters

1. Why do we need to repent and confess our sins when we gather to worship God and receive Communion?
2. Read through the words of the General Confessions below, looking at what they suggest we should be sorting out in our lives. Have we become calloused to any of these, so we no longer count them as needing repentance?
3. As the church community here, what things do we perhaps need to repent of together? Are there any long-standing blocks (such as wrong attitudes, misplaced priorities) on the road which we've stopped noticing because we are so accustomed to them? Get rid of them now by repenting together of them, and resolving to address them.

Almighty God our Father,
long-suffering, full of grace and truth,
you create us from nothing and give us life.
You give your faithful people new life in the
water of baptism.
You do not turn your face from us,
nor cast us aside.
We confess that we have sinned
against you and our neighbour.
We have wounded your love and marred
your image in us.
Restore us for the sake of your Son,
and bring us to heavenly joy,
in Jesus Christ our Lord.
Amen.

Almighty and most merciful Father,
we have wandered and strayed from your
ways like lost sheep.
We have followed too much the devices and
desires of our own hearts.
We have offended against your holy laws.
We have left undone those things that we
ought to have done;
and we have done those things that we
ought not to have done;
and there is no health in us.
But you, O Lord, have mercy upon us sinners.
Spare those who confess their faults.
Restore those who are penitent,
according to your promises declared to
mankind in Jesus Christ our Lord.
And grant, O most merciful Father,
for his sake,
that we may live a disciplined,
righteous and godly life,
to the glory of your holy name.
Amen.

All-age talk

(The president or preacher uses this talk to gather together everyone's exploration of the Word in their groups. During the talk everyone will share something of what they have been discovering about repentance.)

Explain that today we are looking at what it means to repent, but we can't do that unless we know what the word 'repent' means. So first of all the Rocks are going to help us all understand the meaning of the word.

Now that we know repent means to turn round and face God's way, we can start to do something about it. When we look at ourselves and the way we think, speak to people and behave, we all know that we are sometimes unkind, rude, dishonest and so on. Repenting of all this sin in us is rather like making a good, clear road ready for Jesus to get to us easily. The Pebbles show the road they have been working on. Get them to point out first all the nasty 'sin stones' which we want to clear away from the road, and which they have scribbled out, and then all the loving things which help to make our road good and strong.

Here we are as the church, meeting together to worship God and share the bread and wine as Jesus' friends. And one of the first things we do, after we've greeted each other – The Lord be with you; and also with you – is to confess our sins. What did the adults discover was valuable about confessing our sins together like this? (The representatives briefly share the main points that were raised in their groups.) Reinforce any points you want to, and add anything you feel is missing. The Boulders can sum up with their 'Turn your life around' script. Draw attention to the amazingly good news at the end of that conversation: when we repent of our sin, God forgives us, which sets us free of it for ever!

Sunday before Lent – Year A

Awe and wonder

Thought for the day

It is awesome to be in the presence of the living God.

Reflection on the readings

Exodus 24:12-18
Psalm 2 or Psalm 99
2 Peter 1:16-21
Matthew 17:1-9

What does it mean to enter into the presence of God? Are we conscious, Sunday by Sunday, of encountering the living, powerful God of love who drew light from darkness and holds our very being in his hand?

As soon as we start talking like this, we begin to realise how casually we so often approach our church-going. Simply because we regularly enter the familiar building, and meet our friends there, the danger is that familiarity can take over and desensitise us to the extraordinary nature of what we are doing. Today we are encouraged to shake that familiarity free of any contempt, flippancy or carelessness that may have accumulated, and catch once again some of the profound awe and mystery we may have lost.

Some places or occasions have such an atmosphere of holiness and reverence that it is catching. There are breathtakingly beautiful places on earth which reduce people to shared silence after the initial 'Wow!'; there are occasions of worship in churches, tents or living rooms where the sound of worship suddenly dies away into one of those deep silences of adoration where everyone feels bound together in communal love for God, whose presence is tangible. These are in no way reserved for any particular tradition of worship, but, wherever God's people gather expectantly and in humility, focusing their love and attention on their Lord and open to receive him, God becomes powerfully present among them, just as he promised.

As we see in the account of the Transfiguration, the experience is not exactly a cosy one. There is awestruck fear and a sense of the greatness and majesty of God which is all too vast and powerful for comfort, since it inevitably reminds us of our littleness. How can it be otherwise, when we worship the one true living God, whose loving will brings stars and planets into being, opening up the possibilities of all the teeming life we see and touch and hear.

Yet this is the God whom Jesus taught us to address as 'Abba' – Daddy. At every Communion, as we do what Jesus told us to do, taking the familiar bread and wine, giving thanks, breaking bread and sharing it in faith, we receive not only bread and wine into our bodies, but the presence of Jesus, spiritually here among us.

Discussion starters

1. If we really believed we were coming to Communion to meet Jesus in person, how would it affect the way we prepared ourselves and behaved?
2. In the worship tradition of your church, what do you find helps you to feel part of God's people, in God's real presence?
3. Are we expecting others to 'set up' the worshipping atmosphere for us, or do we recognise the importance of each person's committed worship in our Communion service?

Suggested order of service

Things to do and people to do them

The people and priest:

greet each other in the Lord's name
(the welcome includes an introduction to this teaching Eucharist, and the logistics of it, and the artists begin painting)

confess their sins and are assured of God's forgiveness

keep silence and pray a Collect

proclaim and respond to the Word of God
- Exodus 24:12-18 – this is read by three readers with music
- 2 Peter 1:16-21
- Matthew 17:1-9 – accompanied by the Rocks
- After the Gospel, Pebbles, Rocks, Boulders and adults gather, in different parts of the church, to engage in their own teaching on the awesome presence of God as the Church gathers to share bread and wine at the Eucharist
- All-age talk draws together everyone's learning, in which each group shares their findings in various ways

pray for the Church and the world
(the Intercessions are being organised and led by the Rocks group today)

exchange the Peace

prepare the table
(as the bread and wine are brought, and the gifts of money collected and offered, a hymn is sung, the Pebbles wave their streamers and the Rocks their flags. The artists continue to paint.)

pray the Eucharistic Prayer
(the children gather around the altar, holding candles)

break the bread

receive Communion
(as everyone meets with Jesus and receives his life through the sharing of bread and wine, there is a time of worship, led by the musicians)

depart with God's blessing

Flower arrangements

Flower-arrangers create a sense of awe and wonder for today, perhaps with an arrangement near the entrance of flowers expressing the burning bush, together with the title beside it: 'Take off your sandals, for the place where you are standing is holy ground.' Near the altar there may be the elegant simplicity of an arrangement of a few long-stemmed white flowers in a shallow bowl or tray with pebble-stones at the base. Spend some time in stillness and silence in the church before preparing the flowers, and make their arranging a personal time of worship in God's company.

All-age exploration of the Word
PEBBLES

Sunday before Lent – Year A

Awe and wonder

Thought for the day

It is awesome to be in the presence of the living God.

Readings

Exodus 24:12-18
Psalm 2 or Psalm 99
2 Peter 1:16-21
Matthew 17:1-9

Before the service (advance preparation)

- Copy the worksheets and have the children's folders ready. You will also need an acetate and pen.
- Provide small flowers and greenery, small pots and ready-soaked oasis.
- Provide lengths of ribbon or crêpe-paper strips for streamers.
- Prepare candles with card holders for the Eucharistic Prayer.
- Arrange an area where you will be working.

During the service

- During the hymns, encourage the children to worship in the space of the aisle or at the back of the church, waving their streamers in response to the music for Jesus. (This is *not* as a performance, but part of their worship.)
- After the Gospel, gather the children and give out their sheets.

Teaching
Take the children around the church, so that they can mark their pictures as they spot the items shown. Return to your working area and help the children make their flower arrangements to welcome Jesus to our church. These can be placed around the altar. Explain that when we share this meal of bread and wine and remember Jesus eating with his friends just before he died, something special happens – Jesus comes to be with us because we are his friends as well. We won't be able to see him with our eyes, because he's with all his friends all over the world, as well as with us. He's closer than seeing, closer than breathing. He's as close as our thinking and our loving. Scribe the children's short prayers or words of love and welcome to Jesus on an acetate for projection during the Communion.

All together
During the All-age Talk the Pebbles show what they have been making, and different children can tell what they have spotted in church today – bread, wine, water, candles, flowers, a table-cloth, a cup and a plate.

- During the Eucharistic prayer have the Pebbles and Rocks gathered around the altar or holy table, holding candles. Ensure that younger children are accompanied by adults, and encourage those with very young children and babies to be near the front so that they can see what is going on.

Notes

Jesus says . . .

Just before he died, Jesus ate bread and drank wine with his friends. 'Eat and drink this,' he said, 'and when you do, remember me. I shall not just be with you, but in you – your life will be fed with my life.'

Jesus is here with us now

Can you spot these things?

All-age exploration of the Word
ROCKS

Sunday before Lent – Year A

Awe and wonder

Thought for the day

It is awesome to be in the presence of the living God.

Readings

Exodus 24:12-18; Psalm 2 or Psalm 99
2 Peter 1:16-21; Matthew 17:1-9

Before the service (advance preparation)

- Copy the worksheets and arrange a place in church for the teaching. You will need to protect the floor with plastic, and have several large sheets of paper, paint in shallow trays and small sponges in each colour. Provide old shirts for protecting the children. Each sheet has the promise of Jesus already painted on it: 'When two or three are gathered together in my name, there am I among them.'
- Collect together some pictures of beautiful places in our world, and bring worship flags if you have them.
- Have the children's folders ready.
- Meet with some of the children beforehand to prepare the prayers for the church and for the world, based on those below if you wish.

  God is here with us as we worship.
  Let us talk to him now.

  Loving God, we welcome you to our church.
  We welcome you into our lives.

  We want to give you our full attention
  and offer you our love.

  We love you, Lord God! **We love you, Lord God!**

  Loving God, although we can't see you,
  we know you are here with us.
  Please bless the people here
  and help us grow more and more loving,
  caring for one another.

  We love you, Lord God! **We love you, Lord God!**

  Loving God, we ask you to be with all those
  who are sad, lonely, or in pain.
  Help us look after this world properly,
  sharing its food and riches so everyone has enough.

  We love you, Lord God! **We love you, Lord God!**

  Loving God, we remember all those
  who have come to worship here through the years.
  We remember those who have died.

  We love you, Lord God! **We love you, Lord God!**

  Merciful Father,
  accept these prayers for the sake of your Son,
  our Saviour Jesus Christ. Amen.

  Choose some suitable music to be played as a quiet background to the prayers, and make a colour acetate of a picture expressing God's love for us (such as a sheep with shepherd, a place of beauty, or a skyscape) which is projected during the time of prayer.

During the service

- During the Gospel, at the point when Jesus is transfigured, silvery and white flags can be slowly raised and waved by the children. They can also wave flags during one of the hymns as part of their worship.
- After the Gospel, take the group to their work area and give out the worksheets.

  Teaching
  The worksheets will help them look at the question of how Jesus can be really present with us here at our worship when we can't see, hear or touch him. It is important that we address this question thoroughly, as it will probably be in all the children's minds, and it is a good and valid question to explore. Their understanding, as with all of us, will affect their behaviour. Work through the journey of discovery on the sheet, inviting the children to talk about their own thoughts and questions, and to give examples of when they have felt God close in their lives so far.

  Then play some music while they work on their pictures expressing God's beauty, love and power – several children to each picture. They work on this in silence, or joining in the words of the song being played. For the music, use a quiet, reflective song from one of the *Kid's Praise* CDs, such as 'More . . . or less' or 'In your name' from *Kid's Praise 2000.*

  All together
  During the All-age Talk the children stand in the centre aisle displaying their pictures, and everyone in church reads out Jesus' promise to be present among his worshipping people. Then display the pictures on the pillars and walls of the church.

- The Rocks will be leading the Intercessions today. Have some reading the prayers, one or two in charge of the OHP, and one or two in charge of the music.

Can I really meet Jesus here?

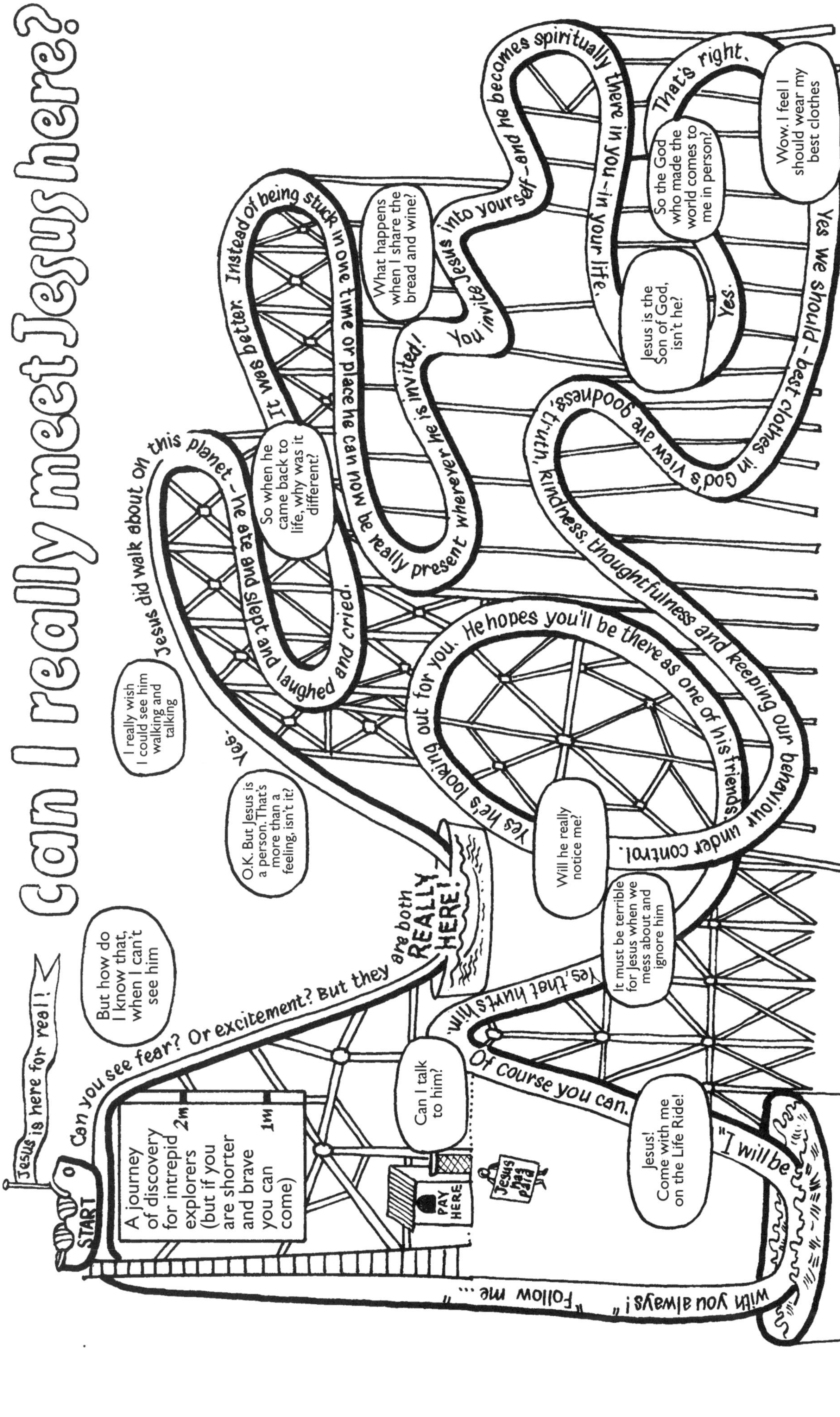

When Jesus is with us, the questions don't matter – he's so obviously there, and it's wonderful. I feel very happy and peaceful...

All-age exploration of the Word BOULDERS

Sunday before Lent – Year A

Awe and wonder

Thought for the day

It is awesome to be in the presence of the living God.

Readings

Exodus 24:12-18
Psalm 2 or Psalm 99
2 Peter 1:16-21
Matthew 17:1-9

Before the service (advance preparation)

- If there are some creative artists among the group, invite them to work on a large-scale picture during the service as part of their worship. This will express the sense of Jesus coming among his people as we share in the bread and wine. The larger the scale the better – several lengths of lining paper could be joined and fixed to the wall, for instance. Use large brushes or sponges for the painting.
- Encourage any musicians to join with some of the adults in preparing a time of worship.
- Copy the worksheets, have their folders ready and arrange an area for the teaching.

During the service

- As part of their worship, the artists begin their painting as the service starts, and continue with it until the Boulders meet together. They resume painting after the teaching, continuing until the Eucharistic prayer. While they paint, they focus on Jesus, so that their painting is a prayer, with the prayer fed by the words they hear spoken, read and sung.
- The musicians – both young people and adults – lead a time of worship using a cluster of praise and worship hymns and songs from your own church tradition. The aim is to enable everyone to sense God's presence as they worship, and this is not dependent on any particular style of music, but the faithful commitment and love for God of those involved in the worship. Using traditional hymns grouped in this way and moving prayerfully from one into the next can be a fresh way of worshipping through inspiring music and poetry. Here are a few suggestions:
  (a) Just as I am, without one plea; How sweet the name of Jesus sounds; The Lord's my shepherd
  (b) Sweet sacrament divine; O adoramus te Domine; Let all mortal flesh keep silence
  (c) As we are gathered, Jesus is here; As the deer pants for the water; Be still, for the presence of the Lord
  (d) Thank you for saving me; To be in your presence; When I look into your holiness
- Some of the group are reading the Gospel today.
- After the Gospel, gather the group in your teaching area.

Teaching
Use the worksheets to explore our understanding of God's nature, the promise of Jesus to be present among us at the sharing of bread and wine, and our need to take seriously the implications of coming into the presence of the powerful living God. They will need Bibles to refer to. Some may like to try expressing awe and wonder as a group 'living sculpture'; some may choose to spend the rest of the service barefoot as a way of recognising 'holy ground' where God meets with his people in worship.

All together
As the priest gathers together everyone's exploration of what it means to be in the presence of the living God, different voices from the group call out the various reactions they have discovered of people in the Bible who have suddenly realised they are in God's presence.

Notes

ABRAHAM Genesis 17:1-3 (draw or write his reaction)	JACOB Genesis 28:16-17
MOSES Exodus 3:4-6	ISAIAH Isaiah 6:1-5
EZEKIEL Ezekiel 1:28-2:1	JEREMIAH Jeremiah 1:4-8
THE GUARDS Matthew 28:2-4	DANIEL Daniel 8:17
THOMAS John 20:27-28	THE DISCIPLES John 20:19-20
THE DISCIPLES Acts 2:4	PAUL Acts 9:3-6

TO BE IN GOD'S PRESENCE

WE MUST ALWAYS BE IN GOD'S PRESENCE – HE'S EVERYWHERE ALL THE TIME.

Yes, that's true. But sometimes we are made specially aware of God in a personal, close way – like when we are praying, or when we share the bread and wine at Communion.

IS IT WHEN WE ARE REALLY SEEKING TO KNOW GOD AND LOVE HIM?

We're certainly more aware of him when he draws close if we're actively looking for him, and want to welcome him.

DOES IT HAPPEN AS SOON AS YOU ASK?

No, not usually. You know how, if we wait in stillness, we start seeing wildlife, but if we crash around, we don't? Well, it's a bit like that with God. Wait on him in the stillness of your heart, and you will find you are in his presence.

"... IT WAS WHEN HE BROKE THE BREAD THAT WE SUDDENLY KNEW HIM..."

"DO THIS AS OFTEN AS YOU EAT THE BREAD AND DRINK THE WINE IN REMEMBRANCE OF ME"

'FEED ON HIM IN YOUR HEART BY FAITH WITH THANKSGIVING'

'THIS IS MY BODY, GIVEN FOR YOU'

All-age exploration of the Word
ADULTS

Sunday before Lent – Year A

Awe and wonder

Thought for the day

It is awesome to be in the presence of the living God.

Readings

Exodus 24:12-18
Psalm 2 or Psalm 99
2 Peter 1:16-21
Matthew 17:1-9

Before the service (advance preparation)

- The musicians – both adults and young people – prepare to lead a time of worship using a cluster of praise and worship hymns and songs from your own church tradition. The aim is to enable everyone to sense God's presence as they worship, and this is not dependent on any particular style of music, but the faithful commitment and love for God of those involved in the worship. Using traditional hymns grouped in this way and moving prayerfully from one into the next can be a fresh way of worshipping through inspiring music and poetry. Here are a few suggestions:
  (a) Just as I am, without one plea; How sweet the name of Jesus sounds; The Lord's my shepherd
  (b) Sweet sacrament divine; O adoramus te Domine; Let all mortal flesh keep silence
  (c) As we are gathered, Jesus is here; As the deer pants for the water; Be still, for the presence of the Lord
  (d) Thank you for saving me; To be in your presence; When I look into your holiness
- Arrange for some small-group leaders to lead discussion in groups all over the church. Each leader will need to have enough sheets for their group, and some Bibles.
- Three readers are needed for Exodus 24:12-18: the narrator, the voice of Moses and the voice of God. These three practise together so as to give the congregation help in hearing with their hearts as well as their ears. The organist or keyboard player may be able to start playing very softly a series of chords which evoke God's glory, at verses 15-17. There is then a pause, and verse 18 is said slowly and unaccompanied.

During the service

- The Exodus passage is read by the three readers.
- After the Gospel, the adults move into small groups with their group leaders.

Teaching
On the sheet are the Bible references for today, and the reflection on the readings, three discussion starters and space to record any notes they want to make.

All together
The president or preacher gathers together everyone's exploration of what it means to be in God's presence, particularly at Communion. During this talk, representatives from each discussion group will be invited to share some of the ways they feel the thought of actually meeting with Jesus would affect the way we get ready for worship and behave during it.

- At Communion the church basks in God's presence during the extended time of worship.

Notes

Awe and wonder

Thought for the day

It is awesome to be in the presence of the living God.

Reflection on the readings

Exodus 24:12-18
Psalm 2 or Psalm 99
2 Peter 1:16-21
Matthew 17:1-9

What does it mean to enter into the presence of God? Are we conscious, Sunday by Sunday, of encountering the living, powerful God of love who drew light from darkness and holds our very being in his hand?

As soon as we start talking like this, we begin to realise how casually we so often approach our church-going. Simply because we regularly enter the familiar building, and meet our friends there, the danger is that familiarity can take over and desensitise us to the extraordinary nature of what we are doing. Today we are encouraged to shake that familiarity free of any contempt, flippancy or carelessness that may have accumulated, and catch once again some of the profound awe and mystery we may have lost.

Some places or occasions have such an atmosphere of holiness and reverence that it is catching. There are breathtakingly beautiful places on earth which reduce people to shared silence after the initial 'Wow!'; there are occasions of worship in churches, tents or living rooms where the sound of worship suddenly dies away into one of those deep silences of adoration where everyone feels bound together in communal love for God, whose presence is tangible. These are in no way reserved for any particular tradition of worship, but, wherever God's people gather expectantly and in humility, focusing their love and attention on their Lord and open to receive him, God becomes powerfully present among them, just as he promised.

As we see in the account of the Transfiguration, the experience is not exactly a cosy one. There is awestruck fear and a sense of the greatness and majesty of God which is all too vast and powerful for comfort, since it inevitably reminds us of our littleness. How can it be otherwise, when we worship the one true living God, whose loving will brings stars and planets into being, opening up the possibilities of all the teeming life we see and touch and hear.

Yet this is the God whom Jesus taught us to address as 'Abba' – Daddy. At every Communion, as we do what Jesus told us to do, taking the familiar bread and wine, giving thanks, breaking bread and sharing it in faith, we receive not only bread and wine into our bodies, but the presence of Jesus, spiritually here among us.

Discussion starters

1. If we really believed we were coming to Communion to meet Jesus in person, how would it affect the way we prepared ourselves and behaved?
2. In the worship tradition of your church, what do you find helps you to feel part of God's people, in God's real presence?
3. Are we expecting others to 'set up' the worshipping atmosphere for us, or do we recognise the importance of each person's committed worship in our Communion service?

All-age talk

(This is given straight after the separate teaching, and gathers together what everyone has been exploring.)

First invite the Pebbles group to show the flower arrangements they have been making, and explain why they have been making them. (To welcome Jesus to our church.)

Reinforce the truth that we are not the only ones at church, but that Jesus is here with us, closer than breathing – so close that we don't have to see him with our eyes or hear him with our ears. Sometimes we forget just how real and how present he is! But when we start to think about it, as we are today, it can make us want to change how we get ready for coming to church, and how we feel, think and behave while we are here. Now ask a representative from the adult group to say what difference it makes once we suddenly realise that Jesus is really here in person.

The Boulders group has been discovering how all kinds of people in the Bible reacted to suddenly finding themselves in God's presence. Let's hear some of the things that happen . . . (They stand at different parts of the church and shout out a quotation each, from their sheet.)

Point out how God's presence has a powerful effect on people – just as it does on us as a group of Christians once we all gather in faith and are attentive to him, worshipping with all our heart and all our mind and all our soul and all our strength. The Rocks have been painting how they feel about God's wonder and glory. Let's look at those expressions of their worship now. (They hold up their paintings, and everyone can say the promise which is written on them: 'When two or three are gathered together in my name, there am I among them.')

Well, that's us, and we have gathered to share a special meal with Jesus. What special meal things have the Pebbles group noticed in church today? (The children with their leader can tell what they found – tablecloth, candles, flowers, plate, cup, bread, wine and water.) As we do what Jesus did on that last meal he shared with his friends, in God's company, and in the power of the Holy Spirit of God, we shall be meeting with the living Jesus, and receiving his life into our lives as we eat the bread and drink the wine and water.

So how are we going to behave as God's people, as we welcome Jesus among us? Let's put aside everything else and worship him with our whole selves – our bodies and our minds, our emotions and our wills. Let's give God our full attention, and tell him quietly that we love him and welcome him into our lives. Jesus has invited us here, and, as the bread and wine are shared, Jesus will be sharing his life with us.

Trinity Sunday – Year A

Baptised in the name of the Father, Son and Holy Spirit

Thought for the day

Each person in the Christian community is baptised in the name of the Father, the Son and the Holy Spirit.

Reflection on the readings

Isaiah 40:12-17, 27-31
Psalm 8
2 Corinthians 13:11-13
Matthew 28:16-20

As Christians we are a community of people bound together by our baptism. The Church of God consists of all who are baptised in the name of the Father, the Son and the Holy Spirit. That means we are brothers and sisters in Christ with every person throughout the whole world who has been baptised – whatever their culture, whatever their age or status, whatever their denomination. This is world Church we are talking about, and of which we are members – it's all a lot wider and bigger than our local parish church, the Church of England or even the Anglican Communion. We have Christian relatives who worship in their thousands under the sky in the growing churches of Africa and Asia; others who worship in the simplicity of isolated chapels on windswept islands. What we all share is our declared faith in the amazing God who is Creator, Redeemer and Sanctifier all at once – community yet unity. Together it is we who are the Body of Christ, alive and available in this time zone, to live out God's love.

Thinking like this reminds us, too, of all who are members of the Church through baptism, but whose faith is barely a glimmer, and who rarely give God a thought. They, too, are our brothers and sisters in Christ, and that raises hard questions about our outreach to them, or even our local knowledge of who they are.

It also raises our awareness of what it means, in terms of privilege and responsibility, to be a baptised member of the Church of God. No one can ever become more of a member than they are by baptism; the youngest baptised baby is as fully a member of the Church as the most venerated archbishop, pope or evangelist. The great commission in today's Gospel was to make disciples of all nations, baptising them, and through baptism we are made into disciples – learners or students. We are to remain disciples – which means being willingly discipled – helping one another along in the faith, and living up to the reality of being God's community of love. Every time we receive Communion we are being fed Jesus' life and strength for this calling.

Discussion starters

1. We are baptised in the name of God who is community in unity – three in one. What does that say about the model of living which we, as church, should show?
2. Baptism is full membership of the church. How does that affect our attitude to and nurture of the children in our church?
3. Being disciples means wearing L-plates. What aspects of being discipled do we gratefully accept, and which do we kick against?

Suggested order of service

Things to do and people to do them

The people and priest:

greet each other in the Lord's name
(part of the welcome is an introduction to this teaching Eucharist, including the practical details of the different learning zones)

confess their sins and are assured of God's forgiveness
(everyone is gathered around the font for this)

keep silence and pray a Collect

proclaim and respond to the Word of God

- Isaiah 40:12-17, 27-31 – this is a communal reading, involving everyone
- Psalm 8 – use a metrical or responsorial version of Psalm 8, or a children's song
- 2 Corinthians 13:11-13 – this includes the Grace which everyone joins in
- Matthew 28:16-20 – gather everyone round the font for the Gospel
- After the Gospel, the Pebbles, Rocks, Boulders and adults engage in their own exploration of the Word
- All-age talk draws everyone's insights together

renew their baptismal vows around the font
(and there may be a baptism)

pray for the Church and the world

exchange the Peace

prepare the table

pray the Eucharistic Prayer

break the bread

receive Communion

depart with God's blessing
(with the words from Matthew 28 and the sounds of the ocean)

(During some of the hymns the Pebbles and Rocks wave streamers of three strands – white, blue and green. The final hymn is accompanied by shakers and other percussion instruments.)

Time of Confession and Forgiveness

Everyone gathers around the font, with the children at the front or on adult shoulders so that they can see. Water is being scooped up and splashed down throughout.

(Leader)
We have gathered here around the font to
remind ourselves that our loving God can
wash us clean of all our sinfulness.

(All)
As we begin our worship together,
we want to tell God that we are very sorry
for all our selfishness and lack of love.

(Leader)
Lord, we know that you are the only one who
can forgive sin.

(All)
Please forgive us and cleanse us of all our sin.
Amen.

As a sign of God's cleansing forgiveness, invite everyone to dip their hands in the water and trace the shape of the cross on their foreheads before returning to their seats. (If there are large numbers of people, pour water into several bowls for this.)

Psalm 8

Use a responsorial version such as the one on page 38. Hymns based on this Psalm include 'O Lord my God, when I in awesome wonder', 'Fishes of the ocean' and the children's song 'Our God is so great' (all in *Complete Anglican Hymns Old & New).*

If you make constellation-shaped pinpricks in black paper and place this on an OHP it can be projected upwards to cover the walls or roof with stars during the Psalm or song.

The sending out

Play a CD or tape of ocean waves – such as *Ocean surf* (Music Collection International) – and then speak over it.

(President)
Therefore go and make disciples of all nations,
baptising them in the name of the Father
and of the Son and of the Holy Spirit
and teaching them to obey
everything I have commanded you.
And surely I am with you always,
to the very end of time.
(Matthew 28:19-20)

(All)
Thanks be to God.

Psalm 8

Response
cf. v.2

Verse

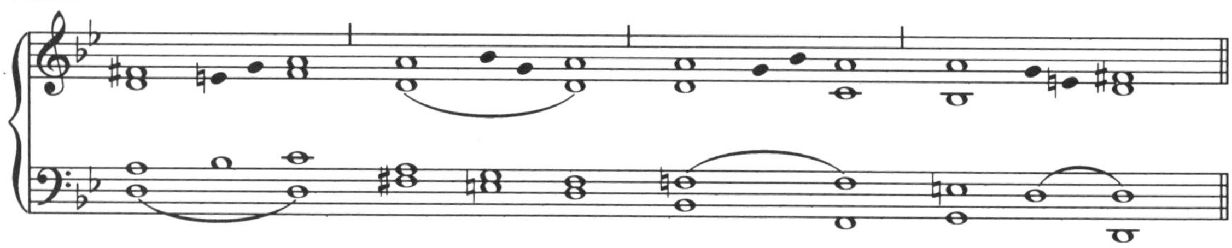

1 *1* O Lord our governor, how glorious is your name in | all the world!
2 Your majesty above the heavens is praised
out of the mouths of babes | at the breast.
3 You have founded a stronghold a | gainst your foes,
that you might still the enemy and | the avenger.

2 *4* When I consider your heavens, the work | of your fingers,
the moon and the stars that you | have ordained,
5 What are mortals, that you should be mind | ful of them;
mere human beings, that you should | seek them out?

3 *6* You have made them little lower | than the angels
and crown them with glo | ry and honour.
7 You have given them dominion over the works | of your hands
and put all things un | der their feet,

4 *8* All sheep and oxen, even the wild beasts | of the field,
9 The birds of the air, the fish | of the sea
and whatsoever moves in the paths | of the sea.
10 O Lord our governor, how glorious is your name in | all the world!

Words: from *The Revised Psalter*
Response: Rosalie Bonighton
Verse: Laurence Bevenot

Communal reading of Isaiah 40:12-17, 27-31

(This version is from the Children's International Bible)

All	**Who has measured the oceans in the palm of his hand? Who has used his hand to measure the sky?**
Women/girls	Who has used a bowl to measure all the dust of the earth?
Men/boys	Who has used scales to weigh the mountains and the hills?
All	**Who has known the mind of the Lord? Who has been able to give the Lord advice?**
Women/girls	Whom did the Lord ask for help? Who taught him the right way?
Men/boys	Who taught the Lord knowledge? Who showed him the way to understanding?
All	**The nations are like one small drop in a bucket. They are no more than the dust on his measuring scales. To him the islands are no more than fine dust on his scales.**
Men/boys	All the trees in Lebanon are not enough for the altar fires. And all the animals in Lebanon are not enough for burnt offerings.
Women/girls	Compared to the Lord all the nations are worth nothing. To him they are less than nothing.
All	**People of Jacob, why do you complain? People of Israel, why do you say, 'The Lord does not see what happens to me. He does not care if I am treated fairly'?**
Men/boys	Surely you know. Surely you have heard.
Children	The Lord is the God who lives for ever. He created all the world.
All	**He does not become tired or need to rest. No one can understand how great his wisdom is.**
Women/girls	The Lord gives strength to those who are tired.
Men/boys	He gives more power to those who are weak.
Children	Even boys become tired and need to rest.
Men/boys	Even young men trip and fall.
All	**But the people who trust in the Lord will become strong again.**
Children	They will be able to rise up as an eagle in the sky.
All	**They will run without needing rest. They will walk without becoming tired.**

All-age exploration of the Word
PEBBLES

Trinity Sunday – Year A

Baptised in the name of the Father, Son and Holy Spirit

Thought for the day

Each person in the Christian community is baptised in the name of the Father, the Son and the Holy Spirit.

Readings

Isaiah 40:12-17, 27-31
Psalm 8
2 Corinthians 13:11-13
Matthew 28:16-20

Before the service (advance preparation)

- Copy the worksheets and provide crayons, glue sticks, blue wool and scissors. Have the children's folders ready.
- Arrange the area of church where you will gather for the teaching, preferably near the font this week. Have a jug of water in the font.

During the service

- During the hymns they can worship with their whole bodies, waving the streamers to express their praise. At the final hymn give out simple musical instruments such as shakers, tambourines and bells.
- The children will be joining in with the Confession, dipping their hands in the water. Make sure they can see the font at the baptism/renewing of baptismal vows.
- After the Gospel, gather the children together.

Teaching
Give out the worksheets. Talk with the children about the font and the water, and they can stick lengths of blue wool on their pictures to be the water.

All together
During the All-age Talk, walk a length of blue wool all round the people in church to show that we are all members of one family of faith – we all believe in one God: Father, Son and Holy Spirit, and are born again through baptism.

Notes

We have brother and sister Christians all over the world

Stick on blue wool for the water

All-age exploration of the Word
ROCKS

Trinity Sunday – Year A

Baptised in the name of the Father, Son and Holy Spirit

Thought for the day

Each person in the Christian community is baptised in the name of the Father, the Son and the Holy Spirit.

Readings

Isaiah 40:12-17, 27-31
Psalm 8
2 Corinthians 13:11-13
Matthew 28:16-20

Before the service (advance preparation)

- Copy the worksheets and provide enough coloured pencils for all the group to use yellow, blue, green and brown. You will also need a wall-sized world map, or a large globe. Arrange the place where you will be working after the Gospel.
- Provide some simple musical instruments for the children to play during the final hymn.
- Give the children a copy of the communal Isaiah reading so that they can practise their sections, check on words they are unsure about, and be able to speak them out clearly.
- Train two very reliable Rocks to scoop up water and let it trickle down through their fingers, so that they can do this carefully throughout today's Confession.

During the service

- They will be taking part in the communal reading, the Confession and renewal of baptismal vows.
- After the Gospel, gather the group into your work area.

Teaching
Give out the worksheets. Take the children through the statements of faith, colouring as they go, and look at the world map to see where their Christian brothers and sisters all live to help them become aware of our membership of the worldwide Church through baptism.

All together
During the All-age Talk they will be holding up a map of the world, or a globe, to demonstrate to the others how widely spread the baptised Christian family is.

- The Rocks can play their instruments during the final hymn.

Notes

Go and baptise all the nations in the name of the Father and of the Son and of the Holy Spirit.
Matthew 28:19-20

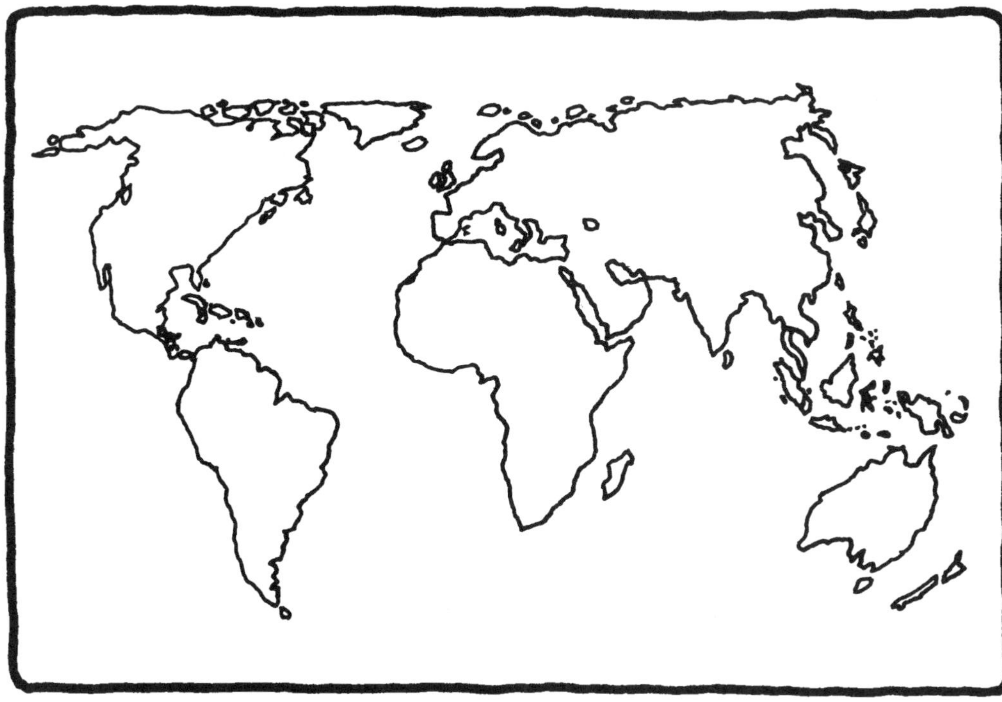

We have brothers and sisters all over the world!

Can you find:
- AFRICA ☐
- EAST ASIA ☐
- SOUTH ASIA ☐
- FORMER USSR ☐

The church is growing fastest in these places.

The biggest number of Christians is aged 22 years . . .

. . . and most Christians are black.

Where are your contacts with them?

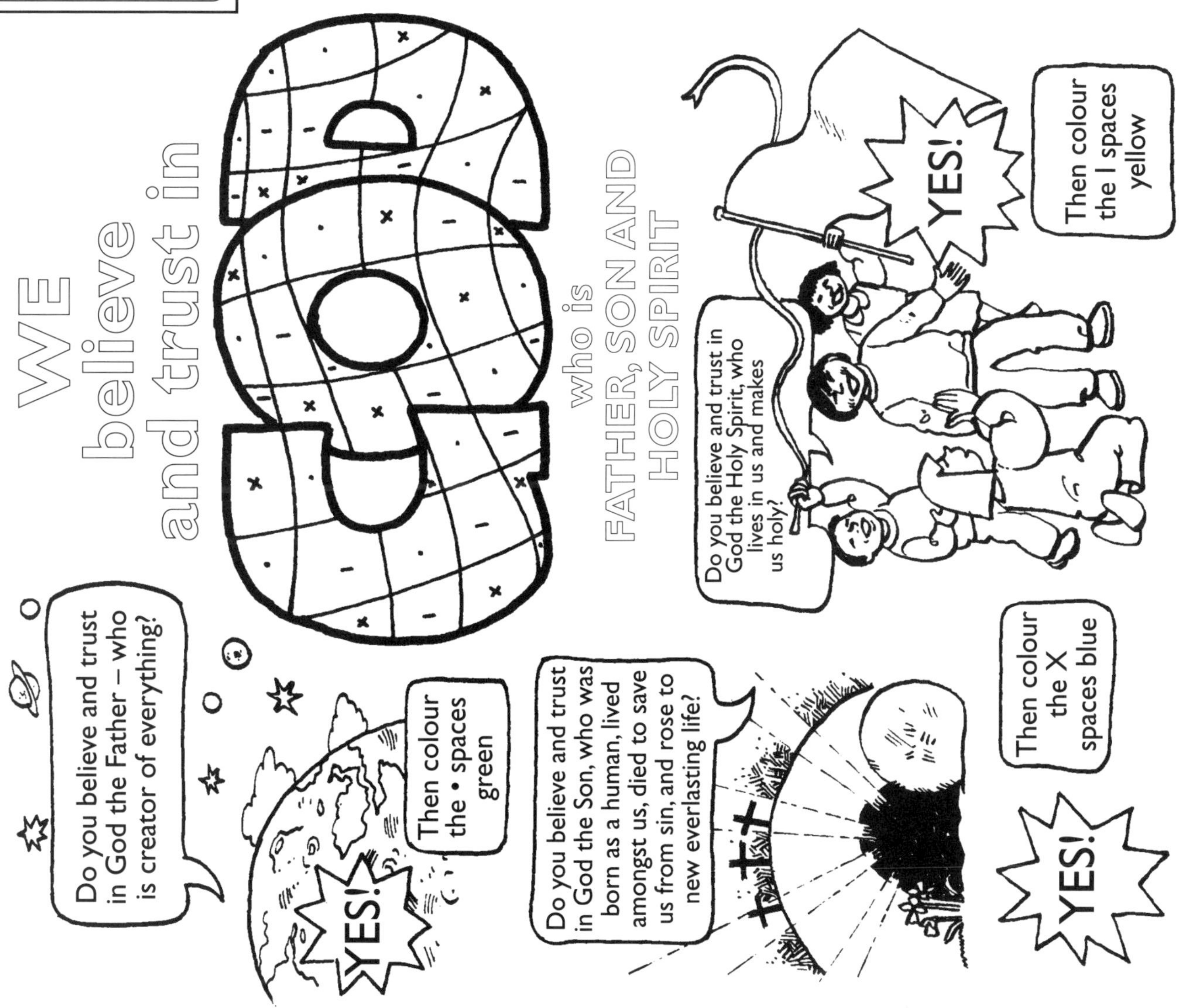

All-age exploration of the Word
BOULDERS

Trinity Sunday – Year A

Baptised in the name of the Father, Son and Holy Spirit

Thought for the day

Each person in the Christian community is baptised in the name of the Father, the Son and the Holy Spirit.

Readings

Isaiah 40:12-17, 27-31
Psalm 8
2 Corinthians 13:11-13
Matthew 28:16-20

Before the service (advance preparation)

- Copy the worksheets and provide pens and Bibles. The group will also need a small candle each for the All-age Talk. Arrange the area in which you will be working after the Gospel.
- Organise two of the group to be in charge of the CD player for the sending out at the end of the service, and practise volume control and timing with them.
- Organise others to make constellation-shaped pinholes in black paper for projecting up on to the walls and roof during Psalm 8. Join them as they experiment and find the most effective way of doing this in your building.

During the service

- The group will be taking part in the Confession, the communal reading of Isaiah, and the renewal of baptismal vows.
- One or two project the constellations of stars during Psalm 8 or the alternative song.
- After the Gospel, gather the group together where you will be working.

Teaching
Give out the worksheets. There is a short script exploring what it means to be part of the baptised community of faith, and the nature of God as Trinity is looked at, with Bible references to look up. Using the symbols of water and bread, they are helped to see the importance of new life, and God's feeding in such a life.

All together
During the All-age Talk, the Rocks will provide a world map or globe. The Boulders will emphasise our commission to make disciples of all nations – baptising them and teaching them – by bringing a candle each, lighting them from the Easter Paschal candle and placing them around the map or globe.

- At the sending-out, one or two provide the sound of the waves as a background to the commissioning of everyone.

Notes

BAPTISED INTO THE FAITH

WHY DID JESUS TELL HIS DISCIPLES TO BAPTISE HIS FOLLOWERS ?

Being dipped in water was a good sign to make a statement that they were dying – drowning – to the old life and rising up to new life in Christ.

SO IT'S A KIND OF SYMBOL FOR THE FACT THAT YOU'RE PUTTING YOUR WHOLE FAITH AND TRUST IN JESUS ?

That's right. It's quite a commitment to be baptised – especially if you're dipped right under water.

ARE YOU A FULL CHRISTIAN WHEN YOU ARE BAPTISED, EVEN IF YOU'RE A BABY ?

Yes. Your parents and godparents make the promises on your behalf if you're too young to make them yourself. They promise to bring you up in the faith until you confirm that commitment at Confirmation.

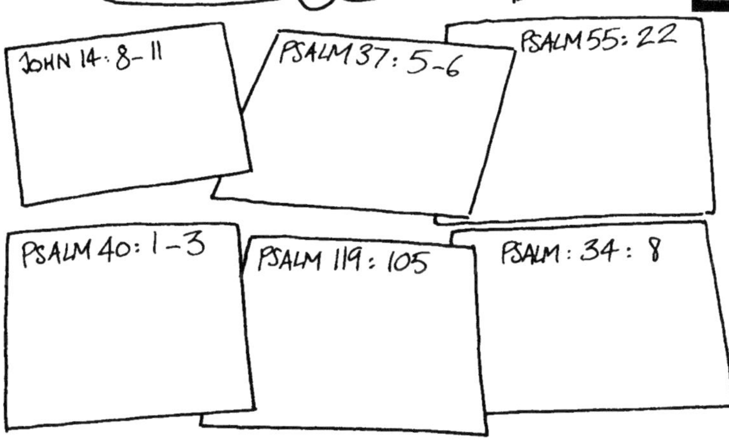

WE BELIEVE AND TRUST IN ONE GOD FATHER, SON AND HOLY SPIRIT

All-age exploration of the Word
ADULTS

Trinity Sunday – Year A

Baptised in the name of the Father, Son and Holy Spirit

Thought for the day

Each person in the Christian community is baptised in the name of the Father, the Son and the Holy Spirit.

Readings

Isaiah 40:12-17, 27-31
Psalm 8
2 Corinthians 13:11-13
Matthew 28:16-20

Before the service (advance preparation)

- The community script for Isaiah 40 needs copying for everyone – possibly on the weekly handout or service sheet. So do the words of the Grace, from the New Testament reading.
- The font needs to be full of water, with a jug of water and several other bowls for the Confession if you are expecting large numbers of people.
- If there is a baptism, the family will need particular preparation so that they understand the baptism will be an important part of the teaching Eucharist.
- Worksheets for the adult groups need to be copied.

During the service

- Everyone will be involved in the Isaiah reading, the Confession and the renewal of baptismal vows.
- After the Gospel, the adults divide into small groups, each with an enabler.

Teaching
Group leaders give out worksheets. These contain the thought for the day, the reflection on the readings, and three discussion starters, with some space for taking notes.

All together
The all-age talk will focus on all baptised people being the community of faith, with the new life that brings.

Notes

Baptised in the name of the Father, Son and Holy Spirit

Thought for the day

Each person in the Christian community is baptised in the name of the Father, the Son and the Holy Spirit.

Reflection on the readings

Isaiah 40:12-17, 27-31
Psalm 8
2 Corinthians 13:11-13
Matthew 28:16-20

As Christians we are a community of people bound together by our baptism. The Church of God consists of all who are baptised in the name of the Father, the Son and the Holy Spirit. That means we are brothers and sisters in Christ with every person throughout the whole world who has been baptised – whatever their culture, whatever their age or status, whatever their denomination. This is world Church we are talking about, and of which we are members – it's all a lot wider and bigger than our local parish church, the Church of England or even the Anglican Communion. We have Christian relatives who worship in their thousands under the sky in the growing churches of Africa and Asia; others who worship in the simplicity of isolated chapels on windswept islands. What we all share is our declared faith in the amazing God who is Creator, Redeemer and Sanctifier all at once – community yet unity. Together it is we who are the Body of Christ, alive and available in this time zone, to live out God's love.

Thinking like this reminds us, too, of all who are members of the Church through baptism, but whose faith is barely a glimmer, and who rarely give God a thought. They, too, are our brothers and sisters in Christ, and that raises hard questions about our outreach to them, or even our local knowledge of who they are.

It also raises our awareness of what it means, in terms of privilege and responsibility, to be a baptised member of the Church of God. No one can ever become more of a member than they are by baptism; the youngest baptised baby is as fully a member of the Church as the most venerated archbishop, pope or evangelist. The great commission in today's Gospel was to make disciples of all nations, baptising them, and through baptism we are made into disciples – learners or students. We are to remain disciples – which means being willingly discipled – helping one another along in the faith, and living up to the reality of being God's community of love. Every time we receive Communion we are being fed Jesus' life and strength for this calling.

Discussion starters

1. We are baptised in the name of God who is community in unity – three in one. What does that say about the model of living which we, as church, should show?
2. Baptism is full membership of the church. How does that affect our attitude to and nurture of the children in our church?
3. Being disciples means wearing L-plates. What aspects of being discipled do we gratefully accept, and which do we kick against?

All-age talk

(This talk draws together what everyone has been exploring in their groups.)

Ask the Pebbles and their leader to start us off by helping us understand what it means to be a community of faith. (They gradually unravel a ball of blue wool to surround the people in church.) Why did they choose blue? It looks a bit like water, and water reminds us of baptism. When we are baptised we are washed clean of our sins, and we are given new life in Christ. Just as we are all together inside this blue wool, we are all together in sharing our faith in God.

What is God like? We know God as the maker of our wonderful world; we know God as Jesus Christ who was born as a human baby, walked on this earth healing and teaching and showing God's love, died on a cross for love of us, and rose to new life so that he is alive for ever; and we know God as the powerful, energising Spirit who gives us God's life and strength. That's why we talk about God as 'Trinity' because 'tri' means 'three' and 'unity' means 'one'. So the nature of the one true God is *Father, Son and Holy Spirit*. (Everyone can repeat this whenever you mention it.) We aren't asked or expected to understand God's nature completely, but we are asked to put our faith and trust in him. And we know that God's nature is to be completely good and loving and faithful, so putting our faith in him is about the wisest and most sensible thing we can ever do.

We are the community of those who put their faith and trust in God – *Father, Son and Holy Spirit* – but are we the only ones inside our blue wool? Not at all. We share this new life of faith with every other person who has been baptised, and they're not all sitting in our church, are they? The Rocks have something to help us get this right. (They bring a wallchart-sized world map, or a globe.) Thank them for this, letting them point out some of the countries where they have discovered they have some Christian brothers and sisters. They can place the map or globe inside the blue wool as well, so that our baptism joins us together with the whole Church all over the world. That's because the disciples did what we heard Jesus telling them to do in the Gospel today – they went out and taught people from all nations about Jesus, and baptised them in the name of *the Father and of the Son and of the Holy Spirit*, just as we have been doing today!

But there are still lots of people in the world who don't yet know God (who is *Father, Son and Holy Spirit*) and have no Bibles to read about him. The Boulders are going to light candles from our Easter candle (they do this) and place them around the map or globe to remind us that we are still being told by Jesus to take the light of God's love to them, teaching them and baptising them in the name of *the Father and of the Son and of the Holy Spirit.*

Proper 4 – Year A

Sunday between 29 May and 4 June inclusive (if after Trinity Sunday)

Wise builders on God's Word

Thought for the day

As a community of believers, our faith should show in how we live, like a house built on strong foundations.

Reflection on the readings

Deuteronomy 11:18-21, 26-28
Psalm 31:1-5, 19-24
Romans 1:16-17; 3:22b-28 (29-31)
Matthew 7:21-29

In today's Gospel Jesus advises his hearers to take his words to heart and do something about them. When we come to church regularly we hear the Word of God read aloud there – a passage from the Old Testament, a Psalm, a passage from the New Testament and a section from one of the Gospels. This pattern of public Bible reading, alongside our regular private reading programme, is there to provide us with a balanced diet of scripture, so that, as a community, we get a healthy intake of the Word of God for our spiritual nurture. Each of the three years in the lectionary focuses on a particular Gospel, and this year we are working our way through Matthew.

At a Eucharist we come to celebrate both Word and Sacrament, recognising the truth of today's Gospel reading – that wise builders hear God's Word and act on it, building their lives on the solid foundation of God's law of love. That way, our lives will remain securely based through everything, and it may well be at the times of crisis that others start seeing the result of our rock foundation.

Of course, it is quite possible to have the word drifting in through our eyes and ears but never making contact with the mind or heart, and we all need to guard against this, especially if we are seasoned church-goers. Even good habits dull the senses if we are not careful. Yet if we stop engaging mind and heart, we actually turn into foolish builders by default.

Our lives are the outward sign of our inward faith, so in a sense we are ourselves supposed to be a sacrament – a community of loving, God-believing people whose lives show what God is like by the compassionate, true and forgiving way they live, working for peace, justice and reconciliation in every situation.

I wonder if that *is* how we are seen? To our shame, the history of Christianity often throws up the shadow of a grotesque God – domineering, pompous, judgemental and out of touch. A god whom thankfully most people instinctively reject. The clearest way those presently alive can see what God is really like is through the compassionate humility and courageous integrity of a people who know him and worship him with their lips and in their lives.

Discussion starters

1. Make a list of characteristics your group has discovered about the true God. Now look at how they sit when applied to us as God's Church.
2. Which passages of scripture do you find particularly strengthening and helpful in living as a follower of Jesus?
3. Which passages do you find particularly challenging and making uncomfortable demands on your chosen way of living?

Suggested order of service

Things to do and people to do them

The people and the priest:

greet each other in the Lord's name
(this includes an introduction to the particular nature of this teaching Eucharist, including the practical arrangements for the group learning)

confess their sins and are assured of God's forgiveness
(the Boulders group lead this)

keep silence and pray a Collect

proclaim and respond to the Word of God

- Deuteronomy 11:18-21, 26-28
- Romans 1:16-17; 3:22b-28 (29-31) – everyone reads verse 16
- Matthew 7:21-29 – the Gospel is accompanied by mime and sound effects from the Pebbles and Rocks
- After the Gospel, the Pebbles, Rocks, Boulders and adults respond to the Word in their separate teaching, in different parts of the church
- All-age talk gathers their responses together

pray for the Church and the world
(the Pebbles place a Lego church, a globe, and a Lego person on three Bibles as a visual focus for the Intercessions)

exchange the Peace

prepare the table and offer the gifts
(with representative people taking part)

pray the Eucharistic Prayer
(the children are gathered around the altar)

break the bread

receive Communion

depart with God's blessing

Time of Confession and Forgiveness

Everyone is given a simple house-shaped piece of paper, which the Boulders have cut out. During the reading of the Commandments, they use this to focus their thoughts. The commandments are read loudly and clearly by readers of different ages, if possible with the words coming from different parts of the church.

(Leader) Are our lives built on solid rock or on shifting sand? This is a time to be honest with ourselves and with God. As we hear the commandments which God has given to his people, let us face up to the truth of who we really are and what we have really built our lives on, whatever we may like to pretend.

(A Boulder) I am the Lord, your God: you shall have no other gods but me.
Amen. Lord, have mercy.

(A Rock) You shall not make for yourself any idol.
Amen. Lord, have mercy.

(An Adult) You shall not dishonour the name of the Lord your God.
Amen. Lord, have mercy.

(A Boulder) Remember the Sabbath and keep it holy.
Amen. Lord, have mercy.

(A Rock) Honour your father and your mother.
Amen. Lord, have mercy.

(An Adult) You shall not commit murder.
Amen. Lord, have mercy.

(A Boulder) You shall not commit adultery.
Amen. Lord, have mercy.

(A Rock) You shall not steal.
Amen. Lord, have mercy.

(An Adult) You shall not bear false witness against your neighbour.
Amen. Lord, have mercy.

(A Boulder) You shall not covet anything which belongs to your neighbour.
Amen. Lord, have mercy upon us and write all these your laws in our hearts.

New Testament reading

Romans 1:16-17; 3:22b-28 (29-31)

The first sentence is written on the handout or projected so that everyone can join in with it, both at the beginning of the reading and as a response to it.

'I am not ashamed of the Gospel, because it is the power of God for the salvation of everyone who believes.'

Gospel

Matthew 7:21-29

Verses 24-27 are mimed by a mixed group of children, young people and adults, who form themselves into a growing house during verse 24. While the rest of the congregation make the sounds of the rain (clapping with two fingers on the palm) and the wind and waves, the 'building' sways a little but stays firm. At verse 26 they start building a little way off, as before. When the sounds start this time the 'building' sways and crumples, accompanied by someone clashing cymbals or saucepan lids together.

All-age exploration of the Word PEBBLES

Proper 4 (Year A)

Sunday between 29 May and 4 June inclusive (if after Trinity Sunday)

Wise builders on God's word

Thought for the day

As a community of believers, our faith should show in how we live, like a house built on strong foundations.

Readings

Deuteronomy 11:18-21, 26-28
Psalm 31:1-5, 19-24
Romans 1:16-17; 3:22b-28 (29-31)
Matthew 7:21-29

Before the service (advance preparation)

- Copy the worksheets and have the children's folders ready.
- Prepare the area in which the group will be working. They will need colouring crayons and scissors, and some Lego building bricks.
- Arrange for at least one Pebble to be part of the Gospel mime.

During the service

- During some of the hymns the children can dance, wave streamers or play instruments.
- The children will be involved in the Gospel, either miming the house-building or helping create the sound effects.
- After the Gospel, gather the group in the teaching area and give out the worksheets.

Teaching

Go through the story of the Gospel, following the pictures on the sheet. Why did the wise man's house stay up and the foolish man's fall down? If we listen to Jesus and do what he says, then we will be like the wise person, building our lives on strong and solid ground.

Teach them the summary of the Law to the tune of *London's burning* with actions to help them learn it by heart:

You shall love the Lord your God with
all your heart and all your mind and
all your strength! All your strength!
And love your neighbour,
and love your neighbour.

All together

In the All-age Talk the Pebbles, Rocks and their leaders will be asked to teach this summary of the Law to the rest of the congregation.

- At the Intercessions, a leader helps them make the arrangement of Bibles and structures as a sign of our prayer for the Church, the world and ourselves to have our lives built on the Word of God.

Notes

1
A wise man built his house on the rock
2
The wind blew and the storms raged but the house stayed up because it was built on rock
3
A foolish man built his house on the sand
4
The wind blew and the storms raged, and the house fell down because it was built on sand.
I'm going to build my life on solid ROCK!
'You shall love the Lord your God, with all your heart and all your mind and all your strength. And love your neighbour as yourself.'
listen to Jesus
and
do what he says

All-age exploration of the Word
ROCKS

Proper 4 (Year A)

Sunday between 29 May and 4 June inclusive (if after Trinity Sunday)

Wise builders on God's word

Thought for the day

As a community of believers, our faith should show in how we live, like a house built on strong foundations.

Readings

Deuteronomy 11:18-21, 26-28
Psalm 31:1-5, 19-24
Romans 1:16-17; 3:22b-28 (29-31)
Matthew 7:21-29

Before the service (advance preparation)

- Copy the worksheets and arrange the area in church where you will be meeting as a group. You will need Bibles for everyone and also an assortment of different versions — both old and new – to show them. Bring a couple of bookends between which are books you have covered with pretend jackets. On the spines are written all the separate books of the Bible, so that the children can see the Bible is actually a library – a collection of books – rather than just one.
- Arrange for one or two of the group to be involved in calling out the commandments during the time of Penitence. They will need to practise this together with the adults and Boulders who are also doing it.
- One or two of the group will need to practise with the adults, Boulders and Pebbles to mime the Gospel.
- Some can help the Pebbles learn the 'You shall love the Lord your God' song.

During the service

- Those who are not miming the house-building of the Gospel will be creating the sound effects, along with the rest of the congregation.
- After the Gospel gather the group in the working area.

Teaching
Give out the worksheets and Bibles. Look at the title and point out that the Bible is a special, holy book, which Christians have been reading to help them know God and understand his love for us, for nearly two thousand years. It is often known as 'the Word of the Lord'. (Show your old and new copies.)

Explain that the Bible is a library, using your 'bookshelf' of books. There are history books, poetry, biographies, a hymn book, four gospels, some letters and some prophecies. Just as we read a poetry book differently from a letter or a history book, so when we read from the Bible we have to know a bit about what kind of book we are reading. Then we can understand it better.

Using the worksheet, look at some different books of the Bible, pointing out the chapters and verses so that they learn to find their way around it confidently. They will be sharing what they have learnt about the Bible during the All-age Talk.

All together
During the talk they will be invited to show the library shelf and explain to everyone that the bible is a library, giving examples of different types of books.

Notes

OLD TESTAMENT BOOKS — NEW TESTAMENT BOOKS

THE HOLY BIBLE (LIBRARY)

QUIZ TIME

How many books in the Old Testament? → ☐

How many books in the New Testament? → ☐

How many Gospels? → ☐

How many letters? → ☐

What's the hymn book called? → ☐

What's the first book called? (It means 'beginning') ☐

Name two prophets → ☐ ☐

Name one of the history books → ☐

'Those who hear my words and put them into practice are like a wise person building his house on the rock.'
Matthew

Lots of different kinds of books, telling the story of God's love.

Love the Lord your God with all your heart and mind and strength…

NOW A QUICK TRIP THROUGH THE LIBRARY…

See how to start a Roman letter

Romans 1:1 and 7
Timothy 1:1-2
Paul wrote these letters

(try starting a letter like this yourself)

A spot of history

I Kings 4:1-19 (you don't have to read it all – just see what it is: a list of names and their jobs)

and also

Acts 4:34-37 (this tells how the Early Christians lived)

some poetry, now!

Psalm 12:6
(What do you think the poet is saying?)

now for some prophecy…

Isaiah 56:1
The prophets speak out God's word

and a gospel

Matthew 2:1-2

which is like other biographies of the time

stories which tell us deep truth

Genesis 3:8-11
and
Luke 15:1-7

All-age exploration of the Word BOULDERS

Proper 4 (Year A)

Sunday between 29 May and 4 June inclusive (if after Trinity Sunday)

Wise builders on God's word

Thought for the day

As a community of believers, our faith should show in how we live, like a house built on strong foundations.

Readings

Deuteronomy 11:18-21, 26-28
Psalm 31:1-5, 19-24
Romans 1:16-17; 3:22b-28 (29-31)
Matthew 7:21-29

Before the service (advance preparation)

- Some of the group cut out enough simple house shapes from paper for everyone in church to have one. These will be used during the time of Penitence. One or two Boulders will be calling out the commandments from different parts of the church during this time.
- Some of the group will be involved in the house-building mime during the Gospel.
- Copy the worksheets and prepare the work area for the teaching. Everyone will need a Bible.

During the service

- The group give out the house shapes to everyone in readiness for the time of Penitence, and help call out the commandments.
- During the Gospel some are miming the houses being built on rock and sand.
- After the Gospel, gather the group at the teaching area.

Teaching
Give out worksheets and Bibles. Different group members look up the Bible references, reinforcing the nature of the Bible, and the variety of books within it. Establish that the Bible is our Holy Book as Christians, and use the sheet to discover more about where it came from and when it was written. Talk with them about reading the Bible often and regularly, and how it feeds us in our faith. There is a brief sketch to emphasise the importance of actually reading it, rather than simply owning a copy.

All together
During the All-age Talk they do the sketch from the sheet.

Notes

A I'm so HUNGRY! Wish we had something to eat.

B Me too. I'm FAMISHED. My stomach's flapping against my backbone.

C Well, if you're so hungry, why don't you tuck into all that food you've got?

A & B Food? What food?

C The hamper of food you were given at Christmas. It just sits there, gathering dust.

A Oh, but that's far too good to open and eat – it was sent to us by the great king of cooking himself!

B Yes, it's far too special. We couldn't possibly USE it! We look at the cover sometimes.

C Rubbish! What d'you think he gave it to you for, if he didn't want you to eat and enjoy it? (*Goes and picks it up, blowing the dust [talcum powder] off.*) Come on – it's food – it's GOOD for us!

A Ooh look – there's condensed milk in here!

B And chocolate sponge pudding.

A Ham, tuna, steak and kidney pie...

B Loads of baked beans...

A & B And a tin opener! Let's eat!!

WISE BUILDERS CHOOSE ROCK, NOT SAND...

WHY DID JESUS TELL THIS STORY?

He'd just been speaking God's word to the people, and he didn't want it to go in one ear and out of the other – he wanted it to dramatically affect their lives.

LIKE USING HIS WORDS TO BUILD THEIR LIVES ON?

Exactly. It was so important that he told them (and us) that if we hear his words and choose not to build our lives on them, we're as crazy as a builder choosing to build on sand.

SO WHAT IS THE WORD OF GOD?

It's the truth we find in Scripture when we read the Bible, and the sense of God's will and guidance that we find in prayer and through receiving Communion.

WHY DO PEOPLE CHOOSE TO BUILD THEIR LIVES ON SAND INSTEAD OF ROCK?

Lots of reasons – not bothering to commit themselves, preferring not to think about it, thinking sand will work OK, believing sand is sensible to build on. The trouble is sand shifts and lives built on it crash.

WHAT IS THE BIBLE?

It's a library of books which tell the story of God's love for the world.

IS THE STORY FINISHED?

No, it isn't. We are the pages still unwritten. The kingdom of God is still growing.

IS THE BIBLE TRUE?

Yes, it is completely true to the nature of God, and it tells us deep, eternal truths. It sometimes does this through stories and poems, sometimes through historic events, sometimes through prophecy.

DO OTHER FAITHS USE OUR BIBLE?

Jews and Muslims share with us much of the Old Testament, and they both recognise Jesus as a prophet. Sikhs also value the Bible as a holy book.

HOW CAN GOD SPEAK TO US THROUGH A BOOK?

The Scriptures are inspired (in-breathed) with God's Holy Spirit. Sometimes the Spirit in us suddenly catches a special meaning in a particular sentence, metaphor or event, and God teaches us through it. This seems to happen in every age – it's always relevant.

WHY ARE WE TOLD TO READ IT DAILY?

Because Jesus saw it as food for the soul – and we need regular, daily food. Then it becomes part of us, and God's word starts to live in us and really affect the way we live. Junk food is no good for healthy spiritual growth.

All-age exploration of the Word
ADULTS

Proper 4 (Year A)

Sunday between 29 May and 4 June inclusive (if after Trinity Sunday)

Wise builders on God's word

Thought for the day

As a community of believers, our faith should show in how we live, like a house built on strong foundations.

Readings

Deuteronomy 11:18-21, 26-28
Psalm 31:1-5, 19-24
Romans 1:16-17; 3:22b-28 (29-31)
Matthew 7:21-29

Before the service (advance preparation)

- A small group takes responsibility for organising and practising the mixed ages mime at the Gospel. One of the group should be the Gospel reader who needs to work closely with those miming the house-building.
- One or two people organise those calling out the different commandments during the time of Penitence, and lead everyone in this part of the worship.
- Group discussion leaders copy the sheets for the teaching. Each group will also need a large sheet of paper and crayons or marker pens.

During the service

- Some are involved in leading the time of Penitence.
- Some are involved in the Gospel reading and mime.
- After the Gospel, the adults form small groups, each with an enabler.

Teaching
The discussion leaders work with their groups using the background material provided and the discussion starters. Write the group's ideas of God on the large sheet of paper.

All together
At the All-age Talk the groups will be asked to share the sheets of paper on which are written their ideas of God's nature.

Notes

Wise builders on God's word

Thought for the day

As a community of believers,
our faith should show in how we live,
like a house built on strong foundations.

Reflection on the readings

Deuteronomy 11:18-21, 26-28
Psalm 31:1-5, 19-24
Romans 1:16-17; 3:22b-28 (29-31)
Matthew 7:21-29

In today's Gospel Jesus advises his hearers to take his words to heart and do something about them. When we come to church regularly we hear the Word of God read aloud there – a passage from the Old Testament, a Psalm, a passage from the New Testament and a section from one of the Gospels. This pattern of public Bible reading, alongside our regular private reading programme, is there to provide us with a balanced diet of scripture, so that, as a community, we get a healthy intake of the Word of God for our spiritual nurture. Each of the three years in the lectionary focuses on a particular Gospel, and this year we are working our way through Matthew.

At a Eucharist we come to celebrate both Word and Sacrament, recognising the truth of today's Gospel reading – that wise builders hear God's Word and act on it, building their lives on the solid foundation of God's law of love. That way, our lives will remain securely based through everything, and it may well be at the times of crisis that others start seeing the result of our rock foundation.

Of course, it is quite possible to have the word drifting in through our eyes and ears but never making contact with the mind or heart, and we all need to guard against this, especially if we are seasoned church-goers. Even good habits dull the senses if we are not careful. Yet if we stop engaging mind and heart, we actually turn into foolish builders by default.

Our lives are the outward sign of our inward faith, so in a sense we are ourselves supposed to be a sacrament – a community of loving, God-believing people whose lives show what God is like by the compassionate, true and forgiving way they live, working for peace, justice and reconciliation in every situation.

I wonder if that *is* how we are seen? To our shame, the history of Christianity often throws up the shadow of a grotesque God – domineering, pompous, judgemental and out of touch. A god whom thankfully most people instinctively reject. The clearest way those presently alive can see what God is really like is through the compassionate humility and courageous integrity of a people who know him and worship him with their lips and in their lives.

Discussion starters

1. Make a list of characteristics your group has discovered about the true God. Now look at how they sit when applied to us as God's Church.
2. Which passages of scripture do you find particularly strengthening and helpful in living as a follower of Jesus?
3. Which passages do you find particularly challenging and making uncomfortable demands on your chosen way of living?

All-age talk

(This talk draws together the exploration of the Word which has been going on in the teaching groups.)

Ask those who mimed the Gospel for an action replay of the house-building, and the crash of the house which was very foolishly built on sand. What we *don't* want to be as a church is a community built on sand! We want our lives – both separately and as the Church – to be securely built on foundations of God-rock. The Pebbles and Rocks know what that rock foundation is, and we can all remind ourselves of our solid foundation as we sing the words. (The Pebbles and Rocks teach everyone 'You shall love the Lord your God' to the tune of 'London's burning'.)

The adults have been scribbling down the things they know about this God we love with all our hearts and minds and strength. (Invite them to bring their large sheets of paper and read off the qualities there.) But they didn't stop at that. They went on to a big challenge: if we are the people of God, and this describes the God we love and worship, wouldn't we expect our own lives to look a bit like this as well? We need to take that very seriously. If we are really loving God as much as we say we are, it's bound to show in the way we live.

One of the most important ways we get to know God is through the Word of scripture. (Show a few different Bibles.) Lots of people buy Bibles and have them in their homes and churches, so that's a start . . . But it's *only* a start. Over to the Boulders . . . (the Boulders do the brief sketch on their sheet).

So it's not enough to have a Bible; we do actually need to open it and read it regularly as the people of God! It's not the easiest book to read, though, and we do need help in knowing how to read it. What kind of book is it? The Rocks can tell us what they've discovered. (The Rocks show their 'library' shelf. Interview them, asking about the different kinds of books there are in this holy library of ours.)

Whenever we hear God's Word, through reading the Bible, through prayer and through the sacraments, Jesus tells us to take it very seriously and put it into action. It's no good reading that we are to love our enemies, for instance, and then decide to go on hating them as usual when we put the Bible down or leave church. It's no good reading that we are to love God with our whole selves, and then spend the whole week ignoring him. Not many people really build on rock; most of us can't be bothered, and go for the easy sand option. Let's change that. Let's be a community built on the secure rock of God's Word.

YEAR B

Proper 2 – Year B

Sunday between 10 and 16 February inclusive (if earlier than the Second Sunday before Lent)

A healed and healing community

Thought for the day

As the Body of Christ we are offered inner healing, and called to reach out with God's healing to the world.

Reflection on the readings

2 Kings 5:1-14
Psalm 30
1 Corinthians 9:24-27
Mark 1:40-45

Everywhere Jesus goes he reaches out and touches people with healing. It is a sign of who he is and what his mission is. The kingdom of God is not one which excludes all but the already pure and perfect, but one where the sick and sinful, conscious of their need, are cleansed and mended, so that God's people are a healed and restored community, worked on with the healing, restoring power of God. Week by week as we feed on Jesus in the sacrament of the bread and wine, we are touched as the leper was touched, because Jesus not only has the power to make us whole, he actually wants to!

In today's Gospel, and in the story of Naaman, we can see that before any healing can take place, the person has to recognise their need. The hymn 'Just as I am . . . I come' picks up on this willingness to acknowledge our need of God's touch on our lives. Or, if you think visually, it is like the Holman Hunt picture, 'The Light of the World', where the door has to be opened to Jesus from the inside.

As we gather round to receive Communion, the walk from our seat is a journey which expresses our recognition that we desperately need God's touch and his healing in our lives, both as individuals and as a community. We would do well to treat that short journey with great seriousness, keeping in touch with our deep inner needs and with the loving offer of inner healing to which we are responding. We come in humility and obedience. It is a simple thing to eat a piece of bread and drink a sip of wine together, but doing so in reverent and obedient humility opens up to our whole community the healing, forgiving power of Jesus.

The healing carries with it a commission. Just as Jesus used bread as a sign to his disciples that he was about to be broken for the saving of the world, so we, sharing in the broken bread, agree to sacrificial, costly living. As we take the bread we are accepting this great commission to become a healing community, through our willingness to be broken as Jesus was.

What does it mean to be a healed and healing community? Again, today's Gospel gives us an example. We are to reach out and touch. As wounded healers we are not to fall in with any marginalising, rejecting or despising which those around us may nudge us towards. We are to be welcoming and open, willing to be vulnerable, always aware of our own on-going healing so that we do not become judgemental or pompous. And we can do nothing of this apart from the indwelling of the forgiving love of God.

Discussion starters

1. Do we ignore injustice, when to act or speak out may make us unpopular? As Christians, in this church, what can we do about this understandable fear?
2. Read through the words of consecration. Notice how Jesus charges us to remember him as we eat the broken bread and drink the wine. So how does that heal, and how does it commission us?

Suggested order of service

Things to do and people to do them

The people and the priest:

greet each other in the Lord's name
(this includes an introduction to the teaching Eucharist and the practicalities of the shared exploration of the Word)

confess their sins and are assured of God's forgiveness
(a small group of adults leads this; a suggested setting for it is provided)

keep silence and pray a Collect

proclaim and respond to the Word of God

- 2 Kings 5:1-14 – this is dramatised using different voices for the characters
- 1 Corinthians 9:24-27 – a visual background is provided for this reading
- Mark 1:40-45
- After the Gospel, Pebbles, Rocks, Boulders and adults explore the Word in their own teaching, in different parts of the church
- All-age talk brings this exploration together, so that the different age groups help one another

pray for the Church and the world
(the Boulders are responsible for leading the prayers this week)

exchange the Peace
(an alternative introduction is offered)

prepare the table
(representatives from different age groups help with this)

pray the Eucharistic Prayer
(the children gather round so that they can see what is going on)

break the bread

receive Communion
(focusing on our healing)

depart with God's blessing

Time of Confession and Forgiveness

(Two of the Rocks group walk round the church with a mirror, on which is written: 'God looks on the heart.' Meanwhile everyone (or the rest of the Rocks) sings the third verse of 'Be still, for the presence of the Lord' ('Be still, for the power of the Lord'). The melody continues quietly during the following responses:

As we call to mind what we are really like
in our thinking, our priorities,
our desires and attitudes,
we long for inner healing.
Lord, if you want, you can make me clean.

As your great love shows up to us
our lack of love, our selfishness and stubborn wills,
we long for inner healing.
Lord, if you want, you can make me clean.

(The Rocks repeat the section of verse 3: 'No work too hard for him . . .')
Lord, if you want, you can make me clean.

Jesus says, 'I do want to! Be clean!'

(Then the words of forgiveness are proclaimed.)

Old Testament reading

2 Kings 5:1-14

You will need a narrator, and different voices for the servant girl, the king of Aram, the king of Israel, Elisha's messenger, and Naaman's servant. The letter is read by the king of Aram's voice. Choose appropriate voices and ages, and enjoy it – it's a wonderful story! Add some actions and props if you like, such as a scroll and some suitcases for all the changes of clothing.

New Testament reading

1 Corinthians 9:24-27

If you have an OHP, project a picture of an Olympic race during this reading. Alternatively, if you have any serious athletes, the reader of this passage can jog in sports clothes up to the lectern to read.

Gospel

Mark 1:40-45

Use the pictures from the Pebbles sheet to accompany the Gospel reading, either with an OHP, or on a flipchart.

Intercessions

Today the prayers are led by a mixed age group, each person introducing one area of prayer. The prayers from *Living Stones* can be used as a starting point. The pre-school children gather for their prayers on a prayer blanket, with their leader.

Exchanging the Peace

The peace of the Lord be always with you.
And also with you.

We are the Body of Christ. Let us pass on to one another the peace of God that we are freely given.

All-age exploration of the Word PEBBLES

Proper 2 – Year B

Sunday between 10 and 16 February inclusive (if earlier than the Second Sunday before Lent)

A healed and healing community

Thought for the day

As the Body of Christ we are offered inner healing, and called to reach out with God's healing to the world.

Readings

2 Kings 5:1-14
Psalm 30
1 Corinthians 9:24-27
Mark 1:40-45

Before the service (advance preparation)

- Copy the sheets and prepare the area in church where the group will be working. You will also need crayons, gluesticks, and the chalice and bread shapes (traced from the worksheet) cut out of coloured paper.
- If you are using the OHP for the Gospel reading, enlarge the pictures from the sheet on to acetates and colour them ready to project them during the reading.
- For the Pebbles' prayer time, bring a blanket or rug which is laid down in the aisle for you and the children to sit on. Have with you a selection of pictures to help the children pray. These might include a picture of beautiful scenery and animals, of children in different parts of the world, elderly people, someone ill or in hospital, and some who are without homes.

During the service

- The children can shake percussion instruments or wave streamers during some of the hymns.
- After the Gospel, gather the group in the area you have prepared.

Teaching
Give out the worksheets. Let the children help tell you the story of the leper, using the pictures on the sheet. Jesus touched the leper and healed him, not just of his illness but of feeling left out and lonely. At the Communion, Jesus touches our lives as well. As we gather to worship, and share the bread and the wine or a blessing, Jesus comes to us. When we walk to the altar we know that Jesus is here with us, and we can say quietly to him, 'Jesus I see that you love me. Feed me with your life today so I can live the loving way.' They each stick the shapes of bread and wine on their sheet, draw on a cross, and practise saying the prayer together, ready for praying it just before Communion or a blessing.

All together
During the All-age Talk the Pebbles walk to the altar saying, very quietly, the prayer they have learnt.

- When it is time for the Intercessions gather the group around you on the prayer blanket, and quietly explain that we are all going to pray. Using the pictures, one by one, lead them in praying, and encourage their own prayers as well.
- Encourage the children to gather round the altar at the Eucharistic Prayer, so that they feel enveloped by the prayer of the whole church, and can see what is going on.

Notes

Jesus, I see that you love me. Feed me with your life today so I can live the loving way.

'If you want to, you can make me well.'

Can you tell the story?

Mark 1:40-45

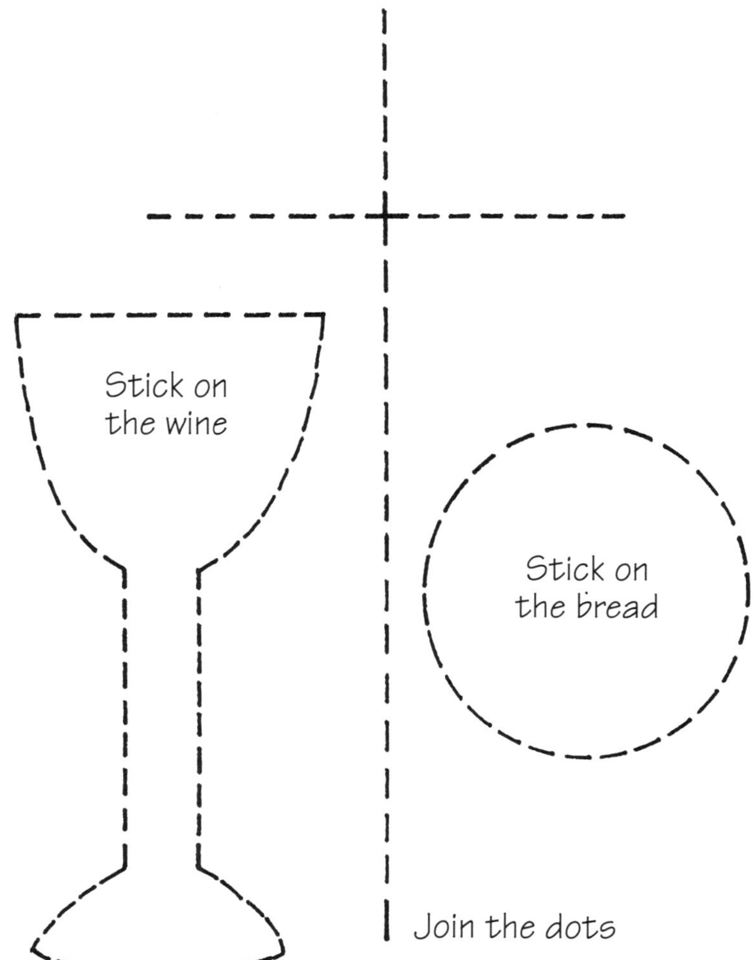

All-age exploration of the Word ROCKS

Proper 2 – Year B

Sunday between 10 and 16 February inclusive (if earlier than the Second Sunday before Lent)

A healed and healing community

Thought for the day

As the Body of Christ we are offered inner healing, and called to reach out with God's healing to the world.

Readings

2 Kings 5:1-14
Psalm 30
1 Corinthians 9:24-27
Mark 1:40-45

Before the service (advance preparation)

- Copy the sheets and prepare the area in which you will be working. You will also need pencils and crayons, a globe, a candle, and some 'bandages' (strips of rag) and a sticking plaster or two.
- Arrange for one of the group to be Naaman's servant girl in the Old Testament reading, and one or two to help lead the Intercessions. They are responsible for the prayers for the world. They can use this prayer from Rocks in *Living Stones*, adding to it and adapting it as seems most appropriate:

We pray for all the people who live
with us on planet earth.
Help us to look after the world we share
and treat it with love and respect.
We pray for all those who are ill, or sad, or lonely,
and for those who no one wants to be friends with.
Please help them, Jesus, and help us to help them too.

During the service

- Two of the group carry round the mirrors during the time of Penitence.
- Some of the group will be helping with the readings and the intercessions.
- Encourage them to play percussion instruments and wave streamers during some of the hymns.
- After the Gospel, gather the group in the work area and give out the sheets.

Teaching
Put down a roll of bandage as you remind the children of the way Jesus went about healing people, like the leper in the Gospel today. Healing people was a sign that the kingdom of God was coming – all the prophets had said that when the Messiah came, he would heal the sick, give sight to the blind and let the deaf hear. And now, through Jesus, that was happening! He was touching the whole community with God's love.

Put down a loaf of bread and a bottle of wine. At his last supper, Jesus gave the bread and wine to his disciples as a sign that he was sharing his very life with them, and giving it up for love of them. He told them that whenever they did this – ate bread and drank wine in his name – he would be really there with them, touching their lives with his love. And Jesus has kept that promise.

Put down the globe and a candle. Every time a group of Christians comes together to pray, and hear the Word of God, and eat bread and drink wine in Jesus' name (like we are doing here today) Jesus himself (light the candle) is really here with us, welcoming us as we come up quietly to the altar, and touching our lives with his love as we eat the bread and drink the sip of wine. We all need healing of things like selfishness and unloving behaviour. Our church needs healing; our world needs healing. (Stick a couple of plasters on the globe, and wind the bandage around it.) And week by week we can come to have Jesus' healing touch, through sharing the sacrament of bread and wine.

So when we come to the altar, it's a time to be very quiet, keeping ourselves ready to welcome Jesus. That means not just guarding our bodies to behave properly, but guarding our thoughts as well. Just concentrate on Jesus. We can think about him touching the lives of each other person in church, and of all the other people in our Christian family right across the world, and in every time zone. And we can welcome him into our own life as well.

On the sheet there are suggestions for helping them respond to Jesus coming in person at Communion, as it is the realisation of this truth which enables their reverence and wonder.

All together
During the All-age Talk the Rocks show the symbols they have been using in their teaching about healing.

Notes

We pray for all the people who live with us on planet Earth.

Help us to look after the world we share and treat it with love and respect.

We pray for all those who are ill, or sad, or lonely, and for those who no one wants to be friends with. Please help them, Jesus, and help us to help them too.

READING THE SIGNS

• Lepers will be cleansed	
• The blind will see	
• The deaf will hear	

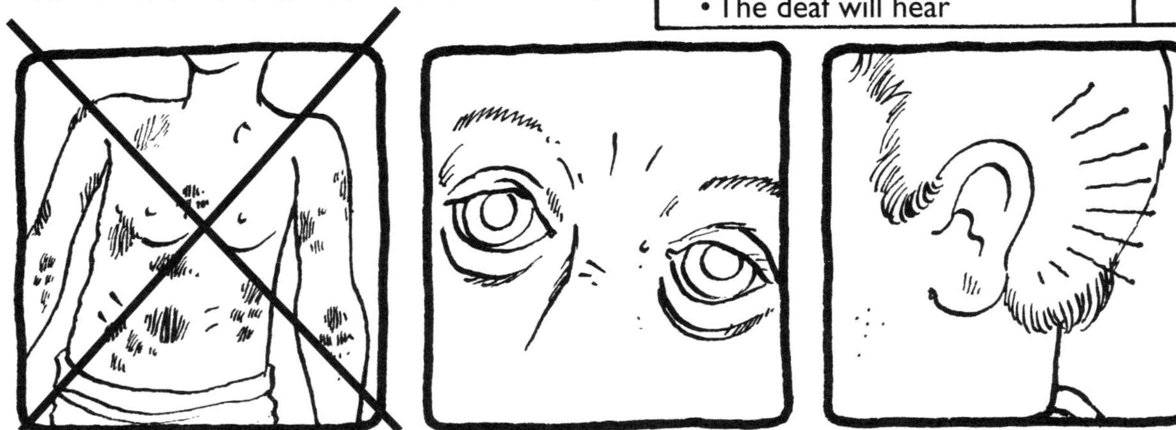

THE KINGDOM OF GOD IS COMING IN !

'I am really here with you!'

JESUS heals US with love so that we can bring God's LOVE and HEALING to OTHERS

• red
× blue
□ yellow
ı green

telling lies?

being scared of dogs?

feeling jealous?

selfishness?

showing off?

wanting what I can't have?

being a bad loser?

What do I want Jesus to heal in me?

As you come to communion, tell Jesus about it and ask him to start healing you. No one else needs to know

HOW TO MEET JESUS AT COMMUNION

- walk quietly to meet Jesus.
- don't talk to anyone else, just Jesus.
- let Jesus' love be spoken deep into your heart, deeper than words

All-age exploration of the Word BOULDERS

Proper 2 – Year B

Sunday between 10 and 16 February inclusive (if earlier than the Second Sunday before Lent)

A healed and healing community

Thought for the day

As the Body of Christ we are offered inner healing, and called to reach out with God's healing to the world.

Readings

2 Kings 5:1-14
Psalm 30
1 Corinthians 9:24-27
Mark 1:40-45

Before the service (advance preparation)

- Copy the sheets and prepare the area in which you will be working.
- Arrange for one of the group to help lead the Intercessions. The Boulders are responsible for the prayers for the Church. This prayer can be used to start them off if you like:

God of healing,
touch the Church again and again with your healing love.

Restore our love for you and for one another,
so that we always seek first
the kingdom of God and his righteousness.

Keep us walking in your footsteps
in humility and obedience.

- Arrange for one of the group to take part in the Old Testament reading.
- If you are using an acetate during the New Testament reading, organise one or two of the group to do this.

During the service

- Give the group their activity sheets as they come into church so that they can refer to them during the readings.
- Some of the group will be involved in the readings and the Intercessions.
- After the Gospel, gather the group in the teaching area.

Teaching
Go through the quiz and checklist they have completed during the readings and establish Naaman's need for humility and obedience. Look at the roots of these words in order to understand them better – humility is earth-based, and obedience is getting into a position where you can hear. How does that match up with our relationship with God? Use the chart on the sheet to think about how we feel in relation to him, and where we would like to be.

Now look at the section of the Eucharistic Prayer where we recognise that Jesus is among us as one who serves. How does he come?

- as a foot-washing servant
- facing torture and death rather than have us remaining locked in the sin-spiral
- wanting to share with us his fullness of life

What does that mean we are doing when we agree to receive the bread and wine Jesus offers us? We are committing ourselves to the Jesus life, and that involves us in humility and loving obedience, and living generously instead of selfishly, so that our life is a living sacrifice.

All together
In the All-age Talk the Boulders share the chart so that everyone can think about where they are in relation to Jesus.

Notes

Round 1 1st reading: 2 Kings 5:1-14

1. What Job did Naaman do?
   (a) soldier ☐ (b) commander ☐ (c) officer ☐
2. Was he more/less important than:
   (a) everyone in the army ☐ more ☐ less
   (b) King Aram ☐ more ☐ less
3. How did Elisha teach Naaman
   (a) humility? ____
   (b) obedience? ____

Round 2 2nd reading: 1 Corinthians 9:24-27

1. How does an athlete get fit?
   (a) being a couch potato ☐
   (b) going into strict training ☐
   (c) taking fitness potions ☐
2. How is self-control like getting fit?

____

WHEN YOU SAY 'HEALED' YOU DON'T MEAN GETTING BETTER FROM AN ILLNESS, DO YOU?

It can mean that, but it's much more than that. Jesus heals our souls so that we are right with God.

DO YOU THINK PEOPLE WHO KNOW THEY'VE BEEN SORTED OUT BY GOD ARE BETTER AT TELLING OTHERS ABOUT HIM?

Yes, definitely – they've got first-hand experience of God working in their lives.

LIKE NAAMAN AND THE LEPER?

Exactly. As a church we can only be a healing community if, as individuals, we are allowing God to heal us!

Round 3 The Gospel: Mark 1:40-45

1. How is Jesus 'in charge' in this event?
   ____
2. How is he acting as a servant?
   ____
3. How does the leper's lack of obedience cause trouble for Jesus?
   ____

All-age exploration of the Word ADULTS

Proper 2 – Year B

Sunday between 10 and 16 February inclusive
(if earlier than the Second Sunday before Lent)

A healed and healing community

Thought for the day

As the Body of Christ we are offered inner healing, and called to reach out with God's healing to the world.

Readings

2 Kings 5:1-14
Psalm 30
1 Corinthians 9:24-27
Mark 1:40-45

Before the service (advance preparation)

- Arrange for someone to prepare the prayers for those who have died, and their loved ones.
- Copy the sheets ready for the teaching. Each group will also need a large sheet of paper on both sides of which has been drawn a cross, with the bread and wine.

  One side is headed 'The Healing Touch' and the other 'The Commission'. You will also need some marker pens or crayons.
- Arrange for people to take speaking parts in the Old Testament reading.

During the service

- Some adults will be taking part in a dramatised reading of the Old Testament passage, using props as appropriate, and one or two will be helping to lead two sections of the Intercessions.
- After the Gospel, the adults make small learning groups, each with a leader/enabler.

Teaching
Remind one another of today's readings and read the reflection on them. Work through the discussion starters, using the large sheet of paper to record your thinking about question 2, either in writing, or drawn symbols.

All together
The sheets which have recorded the adults' thinking are displayed around the church where they can be seen as people go to the altar for Communion.

Notes

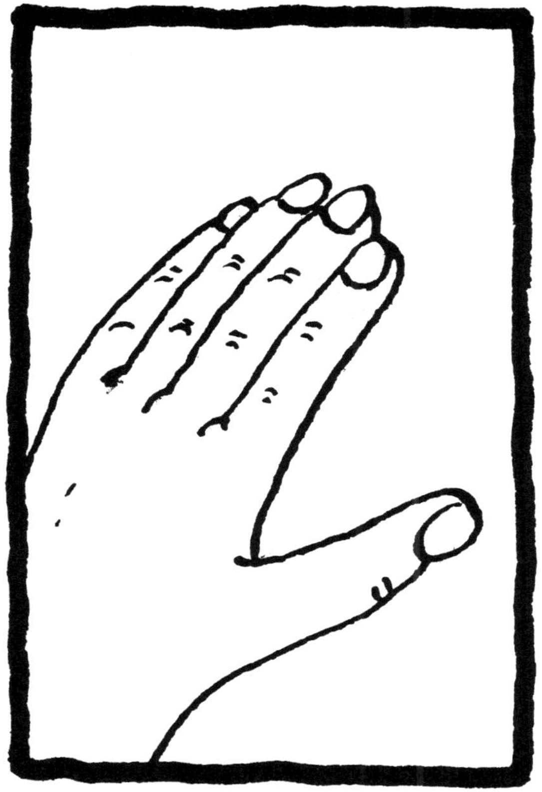

A healed and healing community

Thought for the day
As the Body of Christ we are offered inner healing, and called to reach out with God's healing to the world.

Reflection on the readings
2 Kings 5:1-14
Psalm 30
1 Corinthians 9:24-27
Mark 1:40-45

Everywhere Jesus goes he reaches out and touches people with healing. It is a sign of who he is and what his mission is. The kingdom of God is not one which excludes all but the already pure and perfect, but one where the sick and sinful, conscious of their need, are cleansed and mended, so that God's people are a healed and restored community, worked on with the healing, restoring power of God. Week by week as we feed on Jesus in the sacrament of the bread and wine, we are touched as the leper was touched, because Jesus not only has the power to make us whole, he actually wants to!

In today's Gospel, and in the story of Naaman, we can see that before any healing can take place, the person has to recognise their need. The hymn 'Just as I am . . . I come' picks up on this willingness to acknowledge our need of God's touch on our lives. Or, if you think visually, it is like the Holman Hunt picture, 'The Light of the World', where the door has to be opened to Jesus from the inside.

As we gather round to receive Communion, the walk from our seat is a journey which expresses our recognition that we desperately need God's touch and his healing in our lives, both as individuals and as a community. We would do well to treat that short journey with great seriousness, keeping in touch with our deep inner needs and with the loving offer of inner healing to which we are responding. We come in humility and obedience. It is a simple thing to eat a piece of bread and drink a sip of wine together, but doing so in reverent and obedient humility opens up to our whole community the healing, forgiving power of Jesus.

The healing carries with it a commission. Just as Jesus used bread as a sign to his disciples that he was about to be broken for the saving of the world, so we, sharing in the broken bread, agree to sacrificial, costly living. As we take the bread we are accepting this great commission to become a healing community, through our willingness to be broken as Jesus was.

What does it mean to be a healed and healing community? Again, today's Gospel gives us an example. We are to reach out and touch. As wounded healers we are not to fall in with any marginalising, rejecting or despising which those around us may nudge us towards. We are to be welcoming and open, willing to be vulnerable, always aware of our own on-going healing so that we do not become judgemental or pompous. And we can do nothing of this apart from the indwelling of the forgiving love of God.

Discussion starters

1. Do we ignore injustice, when to act or speak out may make us unpopular? As Christians, in this church, what can we do about this understandable fear?
2. Read through the words of consecration. Notice how Jesus charges us to remember him as we eat the broken bread and drink the wine. So how does that heal, and how does it commission us?

All-age talk

(This talk draws together the learning which has been going on in the different teaching groups, and everyone will also be learning from one another's thoughts and insights.)

Invite the Rocks group to bring you the signs and symbols they have been using in their teaching. It's quite an odd collection of things – a roll of bandage, a bottle of wine, a loaf of bread, a globe and a lighted candle. What have these things got to do with us being a healed and healing community?

Which thing reminds us of healing – or being made better? The bandage, because it binds up wounds and helps them heal well. But it isn't just our bodies which get wounds – sometimes our feelings get wounded, like when we are let down by our friends, or when we're bullied or made to feel stupid. Sometimes our self-image gets wounded, like when something makes us suddenly realise how selfish or unkind we have been, how hard-hearted or cynical, when we had been thinking of ourselves as a good and kind person. Seeing the truth about ourselves can hurt us just like grazed knees hurt when we fall down. Sometimes our relationships get wounded when we have big rows and arguments, and sulks and wars.

Like the bandage, the bread and wine are signs of another kind of healing which we all need – healing which will sort out our eyes, so they can look with love at people and look honestly at ourselves; healing that will sort out our ears, so they can listen attentively to God and to each other; and healing which can sort out our attitudes, so that we know we are forgiven and find ourselves wanting to work hard at forgiving those who have hurt us or those we love.

Jesus gives us the gift of himself at Communion, in the bread and wine, because he knows we can't do this healing – either being healed ourselves, or healing other people – apart from him. Taking the bread and wine into our bodies is a way of taking the person of Jesus right into our own lives. The Pebbles have been learning a prayer they are going to say very quietly to Jesus as they leave their seats and walk up to the altar. Invite them to share this with everyone, as other people may like to say it as well:

Jesus, I see that you love me.
Feed me with your life today,
so I can live the loving way.

Walking up to the altar is the time for you and God to be quiet together. It's a time when as a church we can be quiet together in God's company, keeping our minds and hearts focused on Jesus and the gift of himself he is about to give us as we eat the bread and drink wine. The adults have been thinking about this, and the kind of things we can remember about Jesus. Their thinking is displayed here on the pillars/walls/floor to help us remember Jesus on our walk to the altar. The Boulders have been using this chart to help us get in touch with where we are and where we want to be. Are we close to Jesus, or walking away from him, or too busy with our friends and other interests to notice he's there, or are we deliberately putting up a screen so he can't see what we're doing? Are we listening to him, or telling him what we think he ought to be like? Are we being polite but not wanting to get into a real friendship with him? Are we angry with him for not coming down from the cross?

The globe and the lighted candle remind us that at each Communion, all over the world, Christians are being fed with the life of Jesus (as you say this move the candle around the globe), so that we are healed of all our sin and are free to join with Jesus in the work of healing others.

Third Sunday of Easter – Year B

Jesus present among us

Thought for the day

Jesus is present among us, offering us the freedom of forgiveness. Too good to be true?

Reflection on the readings

Acts 3:12-19
Psalm 4
1 John 3:1-7
Luke 24:36b-48

If we sometimes find it hard to believe that Jesus can really be there with us in person when we worship together, we are certainly not the only ones finding that hard to cope with. In today's Gospel Luke relates what happens when Jesus is suddenly there in person with the disciples – they are terrified out of their minds and in a state of shock and confusion. First they assume they are seeing a ghost, which makes it clear how unexpected this experience was, in spite of Jesus trying to prepare them previously. Whatever they had thought he meant by rising again, they obviously hadn't bargained for him to be as tangible and plainly real as this! Then they still can't believe their eyes because it's all too good to be true.

It's quite comforting to find that the closest friends of Jesus were as rigid-thinking and sceptical as the rest of us, and needed to stand round wide-eyed, solemnly watching him eat fish, before they could take in anything sensible he wanted to teach them. Jesus goes through this performance with amazingly good-natured patience, waiting for the panic to subside so that the learning channels are open for business. All teachers will be familiar with this – no one can take in anything while their emotions are screaming.

Typically Jesus is prepared to journey with his disciples at their own pace, and he does the same with us, addressing first our deep-set fears and then teaching us only as much as we can cope with at a time. (Though sometimes even then we object to the pace, protesting that we're not able to forgive quite yet, or be that patient, or sacrifice so much!) And when Jesus senses their readiness to hear, he explains his dying and rising in terms of the bringing of forgiveness to all nations. Why is forgiveness the central theme?

Guilt and sin truss people up and make it impossible for them to live freely. They clamp us into entering each new experience and relationship with defensiveness. They cramp our capacity for generous loving. They jam our potential for building a just and compassionate society. They distort our vocation as human beings. The suffering, crucified Messiah, bursting out of death into life changed all that. There is, in Christ, a new possibility of being set free, and that is such good news for the whole human race that Jesus commissions this little group of disciples to start the healing spreading out through the whole of space and time. Whenever we pray, 'Let your kingdom come', it is this healing freedom of the nations we long for. And whenever we come to meet with Jesus in person at the Eucharist, the kingdom grows as we accept his risen life through his feeding, and walk out of church freed by his forgiveness.

Discussion starters

1. How have you found forgiveness sets people free?
2. Think about the way we behave at church, generally, and at Communion in particular. Do we notice that Jesus is there? Are we travelling through the familiar outward signs to the inner reality of meeting with him in person?
3. How can we help people get in touch with this inner reality of what is going on at Communion?

Suggested order of service

Things to do and people to do them

The people and the priest:

greet each other in the Lord's name
(this welcome includes an introduction to the teaching Eucharist and any practical details)

confess their sins and are assured of God's forgiveness
(the Rocks will lead this, emphasising the way forgiveness breaks the chains which imprison us)

keep silence and pray a Collect

proclaim and respond to the Word of God

- Acts 3:12-19 – this reading is dramatised by the Boulders and adults
- 1 John 3:1-7
- Luke 24:36b-48 – two voices are used in the Gospel reading
- After the Gospel, Pebbles, Rocks, Boulders and adults respond to the Word in their own teaching, in different parts of the church
- All-age talk gathers these responses together

pray for the Church and the world
(as people lead the prayers, others hold candles, standing in the aisles and in different parts of the church to remind everyone of Jesus' presence among his people as they pray)

exchange the Peace

prepare the table
(representatives help with each part of this, with a commentator teaching everyone about the signs and symbols as they prepare)

pray the Eucharistic Prayer
(the young children are gathered around the table so that they can see what is going on; older children can hold candles)

receive Communion

depart with God's blessing
(everyone is given a few links of broken chain as they go out, to remind them that God's forgiveness sets them free to live)

Time of Confession and Forgiveness

While music is played (such as the beginning of Stravinsky's *Rite of Spring*, or the sound track from a film) the Rocks group bring their long paper chains and wind them all around the church, across the pews, round the pillars and so on. Against the music and the chaining, voices shout out the kind of things that chain us up in our lives:

- selfishness
- guilt
- dishonesty
- lack of self-control
- pride
- hatred
- complaining
- bullying
- winding people up
- lying
- double standards
- greed
- hypocrisy
- unkindness
- vanity
- jealousy
- resentment
- sneering
- lust
- disobedience
- complacency
- wanting what other people have got

The music is faded out into a short time of silence before everyone quietly says the words of the Confession, with their hand on some part of the chains. At the words of forgiveness, all the chains are broken and collected. They will be given out at the end of the service.

New Testament reading

Acts 3:12-19

From the back of the church come the man whose legs have been healed, Peter and John. The man keeps leaping around to try out his legs, and hanging on to Peter and John in his excitement as they try to walk, shouting as he goes about the way he could never walk and his legs didn't work, and God has suddenly healed him through these people. Peter and John are laughing and smiling with the man, happy to see him free. They get to the front and turn round to face the people, pretending to notice them for the first time, and be surprised at their staring faces. Peter reads the words from Acts as much as possible like speaking, making eye contact with the congregation, and walking up and down the aisle (if he is wearing a radio microphone or there are no problems with acoustics). One way of making the reading like speaking is to have the words written or projected at the back of the church, so that Peter can read them from the front, but appears to be speaking them. John and the man are involved with this, responding to what he says, so that in verse 16, for instance, the man can leap around and show off a bit. At the end all three say together: 'This is the word of the Lord.'

Gospel

Luke 24:36b-48

Have a narrator reading from a lectern at the front of the church, but the priest or deacon walking down to stand in the middle of the congregation, and speaking all the words of Jesus.

All-age exploration of the Word
PEBBLES

Third Sunday of Easter – Year B

Jesus present among us

Thought for the day

Jesus is present among us, offering us the freedom of forgiveness. Too good to be true?

Readings

Acts 3:12-19
Psalm 4
1 John 3:1-7
Luke 24:36b-48

Before the service (advance preparation)

- Copy the activity sheets and prepare the area where the group will be working.
- Make a length of paper chain, long enough to stretch round your group of Pebbles.
- Collect a small bug of some kind and put it in a jam jar with a J-cloth fixed on the top.

During the service

- The Pebbles will be helping collect the broken pieces of chain at the time of Confession.
- After the Gospel, gather the group to their working area and give out the sheets.

Teaching
Introduce the children to the bug in the jam jar. He's only being kept in here for a short time, as it wouldn't be fair or kind to make him live cramped up like this for long. He needs to be free to live a bug's life outside.

There is space on the sheets for the children to draw the visiting bug in the jar, and then enjoying himself in the freedom of the great outside. As the children draw, talk about how Jesus wants all people to be free to live as well. It makes him sad to see people in their jars of 'Me' and 'I want', so they aren't free to think of others and be happy, as God made us to be.

The wonderful thing about Jesus is that he loves us so much that he lets us out of our jars of 'Me first' and 'I want' so we can be free to live happily in the life we've been given, thinking of others and working together to help people, loving them just like God does.

The way Jesus sets us free is by staying close to us, listening to us when we tell him we are sorry for being selfish, and saying to us, 'I forgive you!'

The group can now set the bug free outside, thanking God for forgiving us and setting us free to live as loving people.

All together
They will be sharing their pictures with everyone else during the All-age Talk.

- Two of the group will be helping prepare the table for Communion, each bringing a candle.
- At the Eucharistic Prayer the Pebbles can gather around the altar so that they can see what is going on and feel part of it.

Notes

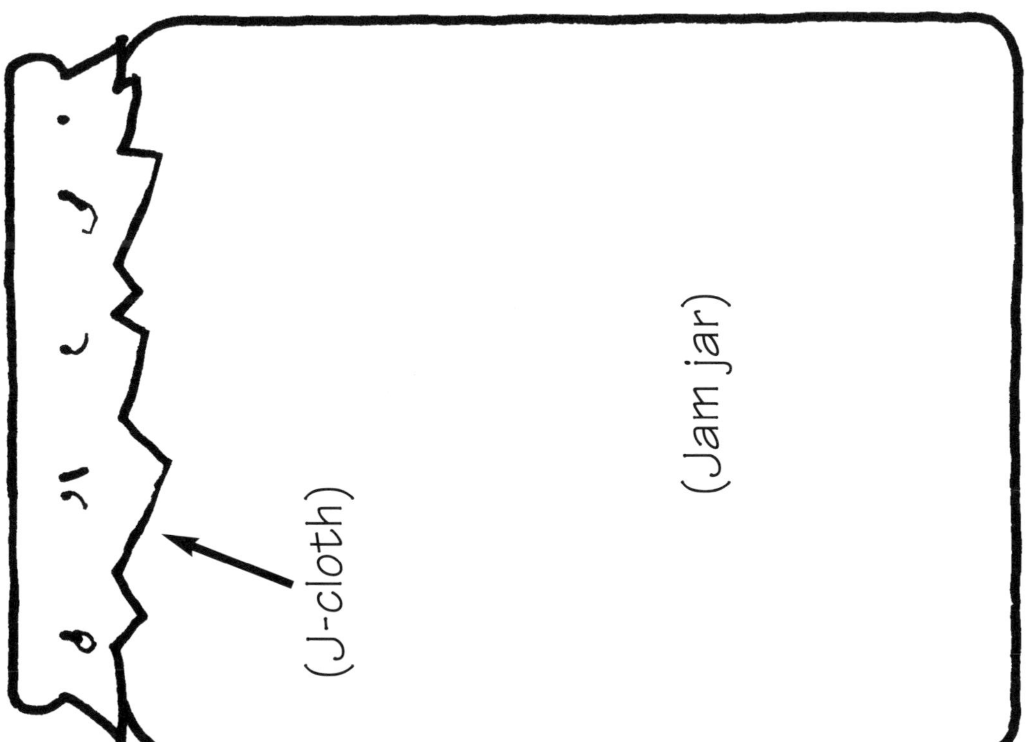

Draw the bug in the jar

Now draw the bug **FREE!**

All-age exploration of the Word ROCKS

Third Sunday of Easter – Year B

Jesus present among us

Thought for the day

Jesus is present among us, offering us the freedom of forgiveness. Too good to be true?

Readings

Acts 3:12-19
Psalm 4
1 John 3:1-7
Luke 24:36b-48

Before the service (advance preparation)

- Copy the activity sheets and prepare the area where the group will be working. You will also need pencils and crayons.
- Distribute packs of paper chains to various children to make up and bring with them to the service. Just before the service, link these together into an enormous chain which stretches around and across the congregation.
- Prepare candles in card holders for the children to hold during the Eucharistic Prayer.

During the service

- At the time of Confession, the Rocks group drape the chains all around the church, so that everyone can reach some of the chain as they pray. After the words of forgiveness have been spoken, and everyone has broken the chains, the children collect the broken pieces and take them in a basket to the cross. They stand at the door afterwards, handing people pieces of broken chain to remind them of God's forgiveness.
- It would be good to have one of the group (a good reader, well rehearsed) to be the narrator in the Gospel. Arrange this with the priest or deacon who will be reading Jesus' words in the gospel.
- After the Gospel, gather the group in their work area.

Teaching
Place the basket of broken chains in the centre of the group and talk through with them the way these chains are a sign of the way Jesus can break the chains of sin and guilt which imprison us, so that we are free to live happy, and loving lives. Place in the basket a colourful notice which reads: 'Go in peace – your sins are forgiven!'

Remind them, too, of the first reading, and how the man had been set free through the name of Jesus. Together decode and read the words on the sheet from Acts 3 – they're part of what Peter said to the staring crowds: 'Turn to God, so that your sins may be wiped out.' What the disciples wanted people to enjoy was the wonderful freedom of being forgiven.

Every time we come to Communion we are turning to God, so that our sins may be forgiven. Jesus has made that possible, by dying and rising to new life. Explain how the children are going to give everyone a piece of broken chain as they leave church, to remind them that Jesus is here with us, breaking our chains and setting us free to live. Share the bits of chain out so that each child has some to distribute at the end of the service.

Now place a basket of candles with holders in the centre. At the Intercessions and during the Eucharistic Prayer we are going to hold these lighted candles to remind us that we aren't just remembering how Jesus once came to be with his friends in the past – he's just as much here with his friends now, as we break and share bread together. Give out the candles ready for lighting later on.

All together
During the All-age Talk the Rocks will show the candles and explain their significance in the service.

- During the Eucharistic Prayer the children's candles are lit, to remind them of Jesus' presence with us, and help them to focus on that.

Notes

You are forgiven!
Jesus is here – in person!
. . . and what about today?
Why are they staring?
Jesus can break the chains of sin and guilt which imprison us, so we are FREE to live happy, loving lives.
Luke 24:36
Draw what happened then . . .
John
Peter
Break the words free of their CODE!
Who has made this man better, so he can walk again?
Peter
John
Jesus
A B D E G H I M
N O P R S T U W Y

All-age exploration of the Word
BOULDERS

Third Sunday of Easter – Year B

Jesus present among us

Thought for the day

Jesus is present among us, offering us the freedom of forgiveness. Too good to be true?

Readings

Acts 3:12-19
Psalm 4
1 John 3:1-7
Luke 24:36b-48

Before the service (advance preparation)

- Copy the activity sheets and prepare the area in which the group will be working. You will also need a candle and matches.
- Arrange for some of the group to join with some adults to practise for the reading from Acts.
- Arrange for two of the group to bring the cloth as the table is prepared during the service.

During the service

- Some of the group are acting out the first reading – Peter and John with the man who couldn't walk.
- When the table is being prepared, two representatives of the group bring the cloth and lay it on the table ready for Communion.
- After the Gospel, the group gathers in their area. Give out the sheets and pencils, and place the unlit candle in the centre.

Teaching
In a led meditation, take them into the upper room, helping them to imagine what it was like to find standing there someone alive who you know is dead and buried. They use the sheet to record how they feel, what they can see, hear, smell and touch, from the options available. Link this experience with Jesus coming now into this room of friends – not as a memory, but a reality. (Light the candle at this point, but don't refer to it.)

Whenever Jesus is present he brings the offer of forgiveness. (Read verses 46-48 of the Gospel.) Why does he do that? Look together at the cartoon on the sheet of someone trying to play football when they're chained up, and talk about the things which chain us up and prevent us from living the generous, loving lives we were designed for. There is a description on the sheet of someone describing how God's forgiveness felt, and a prayer for everyone to keep and use whenever they want to ask for that liberating forgiveness.

All together
During the All-age Talk one of the group will read the description of how God's forgiveness felt.

Notes

SOUNDS	
flies buzzing	
someone sweeping	
a key in the lock	
your heartbeat	
rustle of clothing	
street outside	
breathing	
intake of breath	

SMELLS	
sweat	
cooked fish	
fresh bread	
candles burning	
wood smoke	
jasmine flowers	

SIGHTS	
candles flickering	
cup breaking	
an extra person	
lightness	
Jesus' wounds	

I FELT...	
stunned	
frightened	
out of control	
excited and happy	
full of questions	
peaceful	

TOUCH...	
clothing	
the wood of the table	
stone walls	
fish	
your beard	
your hair	

JESUS IS HERE IN PERSON

TO BE HONEST I FIND IT HARD TO THINK OF JESUS ACTUALLY HERE – I'D RATHER REMEMBER WHAT HE DID THAN IMAGINE THINGS, AND I GAVE UP BELIEVING IN FATHER CHRISTMAS AGES AGO.

Yes, I agree it's hard to believe when we can't see Jesus with our eyes, and no one wants to be taken for a ride.

SO IS JESUS REALLY HERE, OR AM I SUPPOSED TO PRETEND IT'S TRUE?

Yes, he is really here in person – but in a dimension our physical eyes can't cope with. And no, you aren't supposed to pretend anything – God knows all your thoughts in any case, so there's no point!

WHY CAN'T I TELL HE'S THERE, THEN?

Stop thinking so physical, give Jesus your whole attention and really want his real life in *your* real life. Be ready for him to surprise you as he makes himself known in ways you hadn't expected at all.

All-age exploration of the Word
ADULTS

Third Sunday of Easter – Year B

Jesus present among us

Thought for the day

Jesus is present among us, offering us the freedom of forgiveness. Too good to be true?

Readings

Acts 3:12-19
Psalm 4
1 John 3:1-7
Luke 24:36b-48

Before the service (advance preparation)

- Copy the sheets and have a large sheet of paper and a marker pen for the discussion.
- Arrange for some people to act out the first reading with some of the Boulders group. They will need to practise this with the narrator.
- Arrange for two representatives to help with the preparation of the table, bringing the bread, wine and water.
- Ensure that whoever is leading the Intercessions knows there will be people with lighted candles standing around the church during this time of prayer.

During the service

- Some people are acting out the first reading and others helping to prepare the table for Communion.
- One or two people are leading the Intercessions.
- After the Gospel, the adults form small discussion groups all over the church, each with an enabler.

Teaching
Remind everyone of the readings we have heard, read through the reflection on them and use the discussion starters provided. So often we try to live chained up instead of letting ourselves be set free by God's forgiveness. Make a note of people's ideas on the paper, writing the word 'Forgiveness' large in the centre of the paper and brainstorming around it.

All together
During the All-age Talk the group will share their brainstorming ideas on forgiveness.

Notes

Jesus present among us

Thought for the day

Jesus is present among us,
offering us the freedom of forgiveness.
Too good to be true?

Reflection on the readings

Acts 3:12-19
Psalm 4
1 John 3:1-7
Luke 24:36b-48

If we sometimes find it hard to believe that Jesus can really be there with us in person when we worship together, we are certainly not the only ones finding that hard to cope with. In today's Gospel Luke relates what happens when Jesus is suddenly there in person with the disciples – they are terrified out of their minds and in a state of shock and confusion. First they assume they are seeing a ghost, which makes it clear how unexpected this experience was, in spite of Jesus trying to prepare them previously. Whatever they had thought he meant by rising again, they obviously hadn't bargained for him to be as tangible and plainly real as this! Then they still can't believe their eyes because it's all too good to be true.

It's quite comforting to find that the closest friends of Jesus were as rigid-thinking and sceptical as the rest of us, and needed to stand round wide-eyed, solemnly watching him eat fish, before they could take in anything sensible he wanted to teach them. Jesus goes through this performance with amazingly good-natured patience, waiting for the panic to subside so that the learning channels are open for business. All teachers will be familiar with this – no one can take in anything while their emotions are screaming.

Typically Jesus is prepared to journey with his disciples at their own pace, and he does the same with us, addressing first our deep-set fears and then teaching us only as much as we can cope with at a time. (Though sometimes even then we object to the pace, protesting that we're not able to forgive quite yet, or be that patient, or sacrifice so much!) And when Jesus senses their readiness to hear, he explains his dying and rising in terms of the bringing of forgiveness to all nations. Why is forgiveness the central theme?

Guilt and sin truss people up and make it impossible for them to live freely. They clamp us into entering each new experience and relationship with defensiveness. They cramp our capacity for generous loving. They jam our potential for building a just and compassionate society. They distort our vocation as human beings. The suffering, crucified Messiah, bursting out of death into life changed all that. There is, in Christ, a new possibility of being set free, and that is such good news for the whole human race that Jesus commissions this little group of disciples to start the healing spreading out through the whole of space and time. Whenever we pray, 'Let your kingdom come', it is this healing freedom of the nations we long for. And whenever we come to meet with Jesus in person at the Eucharist, the kingdom grows as we accept his risen life through his feeding, and walk out of church freed by his forgiveness.

Discussion starters

1. How have you found forgiveness sets people free?
2. Think about the way we behave at church, generally, and at Communion in particular. Do we notice that Jesus is there? Are we travelling through the familiar outward signs to the inner reality of meeting with him in person?
3. How can we help people get in touch with this inner reality of what is going on at Communion?

All-age talk

(This talk gathers together what has been going on in all the different groups, enabling all the age groups to learn from one another.)

Everyone has been thinking about the way the disciples were suddenly aware that Jesus was there with them in the room – real and alive. And he is here with us now. Even though we can't see him with our physical eyes, with the inner sight of faith we know that he is just as much present with us at this Eucharist. When we gather round the altar as Jesus' friends and recall that last supper and share the broken bread and the wine of his promise, we are as close to him as the first disciples were.

Invite the Rocks group to show their candles, and explain why we are going to light these. When the rest of us catch sight of these little flames of living light all around the church, it will remind us all of Jesus' real presence among us.

What was it that Jesus talked about when he suddenly appeared on that first Easter evening? The adult group leaders bring their sheets of paper which centre on 'Forgiveness' and share a few of their thoughts about why Jesus wanted to talk about this when he met with his disciples.

Explain that when Jesus forgives us it sets us free, and invite the Pebbles to show their pictures of the bug living freely once they had set it free. One of the Boulders reads from their sheet a description of what forgiveness feels like.

Encourage everyone to approach Communion expectantly today, watching with our inner eye of faith to see Jesus and welcome him into our personal lives and our life as church community. Let's come to him knowing we need his forgiveness, and ready to allow Jesus to set us free.

Proper 13 – Year B

Sunday between 31 July and 6 August inclusive

Spiritual feeding

Thought for the day

Jesus is the Bread of Life who satisfies our hunger and sustains us on our journey to heaven.

Reflection on the readings

2 Samuel 11:26-12:13a or Exodus 16:2-4, 9-15*
Psalm 51:1-12 or Psalm 78:23-35*
Ephesians 4:1-16
John 6:24-35

* preferred readings for this teaching Eucharist

Most of the time we are all used to being able to eat and drink whenever we want. Rarely do we allow ourselves to get really hungry, to the point where we are conscious of eating as a survival strategy. Rarely do we face the possibility of death through starvation. Our urgency for food is more usually linked to sustaining our energy levels, and keeping us healthy and fit.

Yet we all know that it is eating and drinking which, at their most basic, actually keep us alive. Without them we die. So it is a wonderfully powerful image of Jesus' importance in our lives to think of him as the Bread of Life, vital to our survival, and full of the wholesome goodness we need on our journey to heaven.

No wonder that the way Jesus himself arranged for his disciples of all time and place to meet him is in the context of feeding, and the bread and wine offered by Jesus the host is none other than Jesus himself. We are not merely recommended but instructed to feed on Jesus.

So what does 'feeding on Jesus, the Bread of Life' actually mean? We can think back to the way the people of Israel were fed and sustained in the wilderness, both physically and spiritually. We can recall Jesus' reply to Satan when he was in the desert being severely tempted during physical hunger: 'We do not live on bread alone but on every word which comes from the mouth of God.' And, of course, Jesus is often known as the supreme 'Word' of God.

Eating and drinking involve tangible, physical actions, and are therefore a clear human sign for us of the way we are to take Jesus right into the very fabric of our being – our physical, spiritual, emotional, and cerebral life. Eating and drinking metaphors abound in our language for the very reason that eating and drinking are so vital for us. We chew things over, find some things hard to swallow, drink in the beauty, savour the moment, feel hungry for love, thirst for revenge, bite off more than we can chew, get fed up and fulfilled. The language of feeding on the Bread of Life touches us where we are most human, so that everyone can grasp something of its meaning – our bodies teach it to us.

If we are fed at Communion with the Living Bread, it follows that as we all leave the church we go out in the power of God's Spirit living within us. It makes us – our ordinary lives and bodies – temples of God's dwelling. Through receiving his life, we physically take Christ out into the world. We walk Christ into our conversations and our work, into every encounter and task.

Discussion starters

1. Do we hunger and thirst for God as much as we hunger and thirst for food and drink? How important does it feel to be kept spiritually alive and in good health?
2. How might it affect our behaviour and conversations to be aware that after Communion we are walking out like temples in which Jesus has taken up residence?

Suggested order of service

Things to do and people to do them

The people and the priest:

greet each other in the Lord's name
(this includes an introduction to the teaching Eucharist, and any practical details)

confess their sins and are assured of God's forgiveness
(an appropriate, all-age introduction is suggested)

keep silence and pray a Collect

proclaim and respond to the Word of God

- Exodus 16:2-4, 9-15 – this is acted out by a mixed age-group
- Ephesians 4:1-16
- John 6:24-35 – the Gospel is read communally
- After the Gospel, Pebbles, Rocks, Boulders and adults explore and respond to the Word of God in their separate groups, in different parts of the church
- All-age talk gathers and focuses these responses

pray for the Church and the world
(this time of prayer is led by the Rocks)

exchange the Peace

prepare the table
(a freshly baked loaf is used for the Communion, and an arrangement of wheat, bread, wine and grapes placed nearby)

pray the Eucharistic Prayer
(with the children gathered round so that they can see)

receive Communion

depart with God's blessing

Flower arrangement

Make the arrangement in a shallow basket lined with a napkin, with a bunch of wheat and grapes, bottle of wine and loaf of bread. Small posies of simple summer flowers are lodged in between. The arrangement is placed near the entrance to the church as people come in, and at the offertory it is placed near the altar so that people see it as they come to receive Communion.

Time of Confession and Forgiveness

This starts on the previous evening. On the previous week's handout suggest that as many people as possible come to church fasting from Saturday night this week, praying the first two lines of this prayer whenever their body nudges them with hunger:

As our bodies have been hungering for food,
so our souls hunger for you, O God.

We are very sorry for our lack of love and faith,
our lack of generosity,
our lack of thankfulness.
We hunger for your forgiveness.

We are very sorry for wanting our own way,
for grumbling and criticising,
for making others feel small.
We hunger for your forgiveness.

As our bodies have been hungering for food,
so our souls hunger for you, O God.

(Everyone is assured of God's forgiveness)

Old Testament reading

Exodus 16:2-4, 9-15

Have a small group of young children, older children, young people and adults. Provide small tubs for the smallest children, larger ones for the larger, and very large ones for the tallest adults. Make placards for the people to display, saying things like 'It's not fair'; 'Down with the desert' 'Egypt: food, Desert: nil'; 'We want food!'

As the reading begins, the people walk up and down with their complaints. When Aaron calls them (verse 6) they gather at the front and start to look hopeful. At verse 13 everyone looks up, shading their eyes and pointing at the quails, and the pointing is directed across the sky and then down to the ground. The narrator pauses in the middle of verse 13 for this. Then everyone sets off with their appropriate sized pots to pretend they are gathering the manna from all over the church. At verse 16 they bring their pots up to the front and hold them up, looking happy.

Gospel

John 6:24-35

Have this written out in full, on sheets for everyone or on an OHP, with the crowd's words in bold type for the whole congregation to join in. Have one person to read the words of Jesus and another to be the narrator.

Intercessions

Gather the Pebbles group on to a prayer mat or blanket during this time of prayer. Their leader has a loaf of bread and some wheat, and guides them to thank God for the way we are fed, and to pray for those who are hungry in different parts of the world.

The rest of the congregation can use the Intercessions from *Living Stones*, or this litany:

The church is hungry for deeper faith
and Christians hunger to know God's will.
Feed us, Father, with the Bread of Life.

The world is hungry for peace and justice,
the poor are hungry for freedom and food.
Feed us, Father, with the Bread of Life.

People are hungry for love and affection,
so many hunger for someone to trust.
Feed us, Father, with the Bread of Life.

There are many who hunger for health and wholeness,
freedom from pain or sorrow or doubt.
Feed us, Father, with the Bread of Life.

The dying are hungry for life which is lasting,
life which is stronger than death of the body.
Feed us, Father, with the Bread of Life.

All of us hunger for God's life within us,
blessing our living and guiding our feet.
Feed us, Father, with the Bread of Life.

All-age exploration of the Word PEBBLES

Proper 13 – Year B

Sunday between 31 July and 6 August inclusive

Spiritual feeding

Thought for the day

Jesus is the Bread of Life who satisfies our hunger and sustains us on our journey to heaven.

Readings

2 Samuel 11:26-12:13a or Exodus 16:2-4, 9-15*
Psalm 51:1-12 or Psalm 78:23-35*
Ephesians 4:1-16
John 6:24-35

* preferred readings for this teaching Eucharist

Before the service (advance preparation)

- Copy the activity sheets and prepare the work area. Have some mixed bread dough ready for shaping, and paper plates for the children to work on. Cut lengths of crepe paper streamers for the children to wave in some of the hymns.
- Arrange for two or three of the group to take part in the Old Testament reading, providing them with pots in which to collect their manna, helping them prepare the necessary posters and so on. They will not have any lines to learn.

During the service

- A few of the children will be miming the reading from Exodus.
- During some of the hymns encourage the children to dance and wave their streamers – *not* as a performance, in view of everyone, but worshipping God through their dancing and waving.
- After the Gospel, gather the group into the work area.

Teaching
Share out the dough between the children. They all shape a small loaf of bread, ready to be baked somewhere nearby, and distributed after the service. On the sheet is a place mat for the children to use for their bread.

As you work, talk about how we all need to eat to live, how our bodies tell us when we are hungry so that we make sure they are given the food they need, and how Jesus called himself the Bread of Life to explain how much we need him, and how good he is for us.

If there is time, they can colour in their place mats.

All together
Whoever is giving the All-age Talk will be referring to the bread the Pebbles have been baking for today's Communion.

- During the Intercessions the children come to sit on the prayer mat with their leader, where they are led in prayer, using a loaf of bread as their focus.
- At the Eucharistic Prayer make sure the children are able to see and feel part of the worshipping family.

Notes

Jesus said
'I am the Bread of Life'

All-age exploration of the Word ROCKS

Proper 13 – Year B

Sunday between 31 July and 6 August inclusive

Spiritual feeding

Thought for the day

Jesus is the Bread of Life who satisfies our hunger and sustains us on our journey to heaven.

Readings

2 Samuel 11:26-12:13a or Exodus 16:2-4, 9-15*
Psalm 51:1-12 or Psalm 78:23-35*
Ephesians 4:1-16
John 6:24-35

* preferred readings for this teaching Eucharist

Before the service (advance preparation)

- Copy the activity sheets and prepare the area where you will be working. Write the words 'I am the Bread of Life. Whoever comes to me will never be hungry – John 6, verse 35' on separate pieces of card. On the reverse number the words in order.
- Arrange for a few of the group to help mime the first reading.
- Arrange for two of the group to lead the Intercessions, helping them practise reading so that it is clear and slow, with space for people to think and pray.

During the service

- A few will be involved with miming the first reading.
- Readers will be joining in the Gospel reading as part of the crowd with the adults.
- After the Gospel, gather the group in their work area.

Teaching
Lay down the cards, number side up. Invite the children to take it in turn to reveal one of the words to find a message we have heard this morning in the Gospel. As each card is turned over, the growing message is read, so that by the end it will have been almost learnt by heart already. At this point introduce the challenge of learning the words off by heart, and do this by saying it over together, each time turning over the end card, until the whole message is being said with no words to help.

Now give out the sheets, where they will find a puzzle with this same text as the solution, so that their learning is reinforced. There are also links made between the feeding, nourishment, and life-sustaining properties of bread, and the spiritual life-sustaining of Jesus.

All together
During the All-age Talk the Rocks will share with the rest of the congregation the Bible verse they have been learning, placing the cards in the aisle for people to walk on.

- Two of the group are leading the Intercessions.

Notes

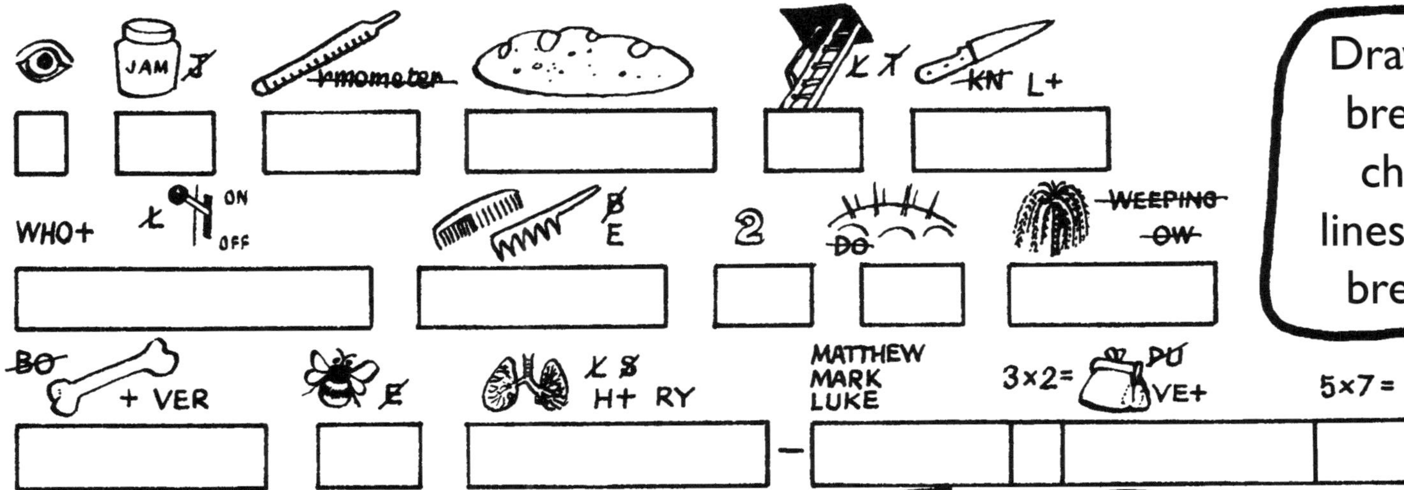

Draw RED lines from the bread to the words you choose. Draw GREEN lines from the communion bread to the words you choose. Some words will have both lines to them.

All-age exploration of the Word
BOULDERS

Proper 13 – Year B

Sunday between 31 July and 6 August inclusive

Spiritual feeding

Thought for the day

Jesus is the Bread of Life who satisfies our hunger and sustains us on our journey to heaven.

Readings

2 Samuel 11:26-12:13a or Exodus 16:2-4, 9-15*
Psalm 51:1-12 or Psalm 78:23-35*
Ephesians 4:1-16
John 6:24-35

* preferred readings for this teaching Eucharist

Before the service (advance preparation)

- Copy the sheets and prepare the work area.
- Arrange for several of the group to take part in the miming of the first reading, and to make the protest slogans for it (see page 89).
- If you are using an OHP for the Gospel reading, arrange for one of the group to take care of the projection for this.

During the service

- Several of the group will be miming the first reading.
- They will all be involved with the communal reading of the Gospel.
- After the Gospel, gather the group in their area and give out the sheets.

Teaching
On the sheet they can record around the word 'Feeding' anything in either of the readings which mentions any kind of feeding. Talk together about the things they have found, sorting them into physical and spiritual feeding, so that they can see how God's practical providing in the desert and in the feeding of the 5000 was food both for body and spirit.

Go on to unpack the meaning of Jesus calling himself the Bread of Life, and the implications of this in us receiving Communion. There are references provided to help their thinking, and some visual hints as well. It may also help to use the words of a Communion hymn, reading them for the meaning, rather than singing. Choose one which reflects your tradition and is well loved by your church. (Possible choices: Verses 3, 4 and 5 of 'Now, my tongue, the mystery telling'; 'Broken for me, broken for you'; 'Thee we adore, O hidden Saviour, thee'; 'This is my body, broken for you'; 'Father of life, draw me closer'.)

All together
The conversation on the sheet will be read out during the All-age Talk.

Notes

I AM THE BREAD OF LIFE

IT SOUNDS A BIT STRANGE TO CALL YOURSELF BREAD. WHAT WAS JESUS GETTING AT?

Well, as humans, something we *all* have in common is the need to eat, isn't it?

SO JESUS IS TELLING US WE NEED HIM TO LIVE, IS HE?

For full, spiritual life, yes, and for spiritual strength, growth and energy.

WHEN WE EAT THE BREAD AT COMMUNION IT'S NOT SO MUCH THE BREAD WE'RE EATING, AS SHARING JESUS' LIFE.

Yes, we 'feed on him in our hearts by faith with thanksgiving'.

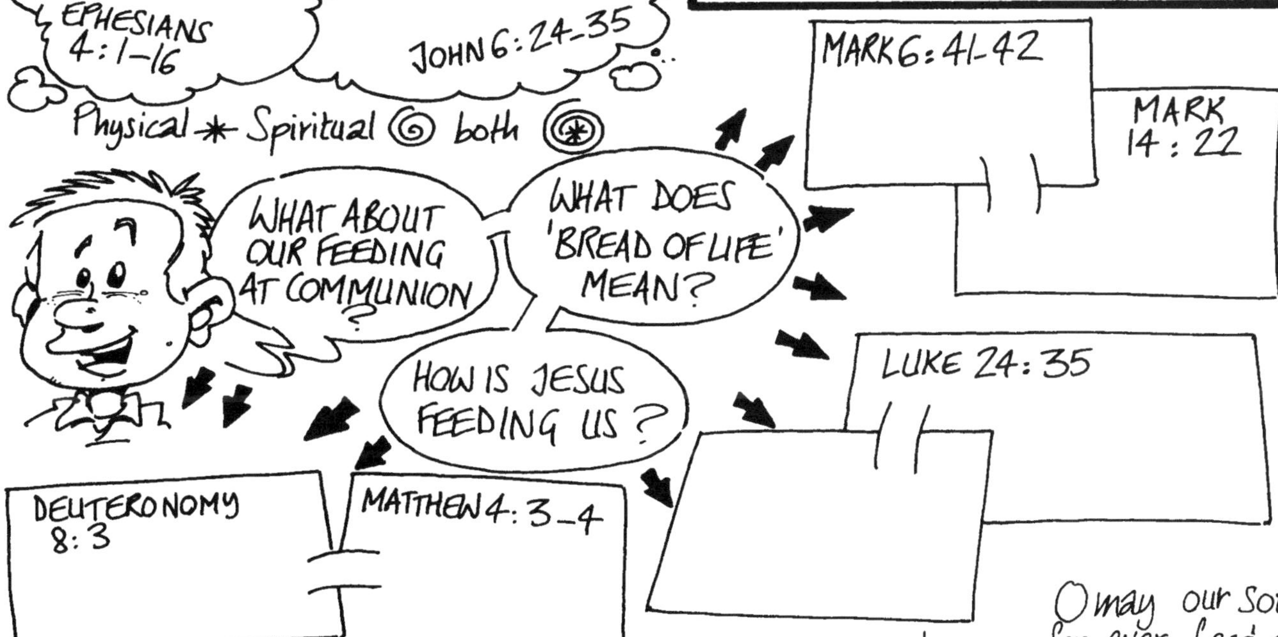

O may our souls for ever feed on thee...

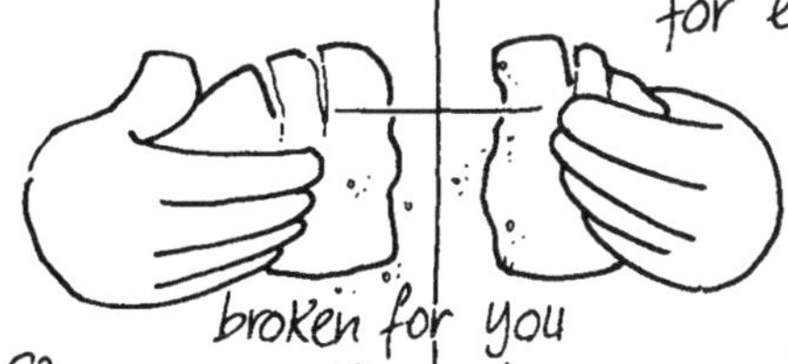

O may we all one bread, one body be...

INTO YOUR PRESENCE YOU DRAW US...

FEED ME TILL I WANT NO MORE...

All-age exploration of the Word ADULTS

Proper 13 – Year B

Sunday between 31 July and 6 August inclusive

Spiritual feeding

Thought for the day

Jesus is the Bread of Life who satisfies our hunger and sustains us on our journey to heaven.

Readings

2 Samuel 11:26-12:13a or Exodus 16:2-4, 9-15*
Psalm 51:1-12 or Psalm 78:23-35*
Ephesians 4:1-16
John 6:24-35

* preferred readings for this teaching Eucharist

Before the service (advance preparation)

- Copy the sheets and prepare a flipchart page with a loaf of bread drawn in the centre.
- Arrange for someone to organise and direct the miming of the first reading (Exodus) and several adults to participate. The Boulders are preparing the protest slogans, and people of all ages will be involved in the acting.
- Arrange for one person to lead the time of Confession and another to prepare the flower arrangement and move it during the offertory from near the door to near the altar.
- Arrange for someone to bake a loaf of bread for Communion today.

During the service

- One person leads the time of Confession.
- The reading from Exodus is acted out involving all age groups.
- Everyone is involved with the communal reading of the Gospel, speaking the words of the crowd.
- After the Gospel, the adults break into small discussion groups, each with an enabler. Give out the sheets.

Teaching
Talk over the readings and look at the reflection. Use the discussion starters to explore the implications of today's readings, and the meaning of Jesus as 'Bread of Life'. Keep track of the conversation on the flipchart paper, around the picture of bread.

All together
The adults will be invited to share some of their thinking during the All-age Talk.

Notes

Spiritual feeding

Thought for the day

Jesus is the Bread of Life who satisfies our hunger and sustains us on our journey to heaven.

Reflection on the readings

2 Samuel 11:26-12:13a or
Exodus 16:2-4, 9-15*
Psalm 51:1-12 or Psalm 78:23-35*
Ephesians 4:1-16
John 6:24-35

* preferred readings for this teaching Eucharist

Most of the time we are all used to being able to eat and drink whenever we want. Rarely do we allow ourselves to get really hungry, to the point where we are conscious of eating as a survival strategy. Rarely do we face the possibility of death through starvation. Our urgency for food is more usually linked to sustaining our energy levels, and keeping us healthy and fit.

Yet we all know that it is eating and drinking which, at their most basic, actually keep us alive. Without them we die. So it is a wonderfully powerful image of Jesus' importance in our lives to think of him as the Bread of Life, vital to our survival, and full of the wholesome goodness we need on our journey to heaven.

No wonder that the way Jesus himself arranged for his disciples of all time and place to meet him is in the context of feeding, and the bread and wine offered by Jesus the host is none other than Jesus himself. We are not merely recommended but instructed to feed on Jesus.

So what does 'feeding on Jesus, the Bread of Life' actually mean? We can think back to the way the people of Israel were fed and sustained in the wilderness, both physically and spiritually. We can recall Jesus' reply to Satan when he was in the desert being severely tempted during physical hunger: 'We do not live on bread alone but on every word which comes from the mouth of God.' And, of course, Jesus is often known as the supreme 'Word' of God.

Eating and drinking involve tangible, physical actions, and are therefore a clear human sign for us of the way we are to take Jesus right into the very fabric of our being – our physical, spiritual, emotional, and cerebral life. Eating and drinking metaphors abound in our language for the very reason that eating and drinking are so vital for us. We chew things over, find some things hard to swallow, drink in the beauty, savour the moment, feel hungry for love, thirst for revenge, bite off more than we can chew, get fed up and fulfilled. The language of feeding on the Bread of Life touches us where we are most human, so that everyone can grasp something of its meaning – our bodies teach it to us.

If we are fed at Communion with the Living Bread, it follows that as we all leave the church we go out in the power of God's Spirit living within us. It makes us – our ordinary lives and bodies – temples of God's dwelling. Through receiving his life, we physically take Christ out into the world. We walk Christ into our conversations and our work, into every encounter and task.

Discussion starters

1. Do we hunger and thirst for God as much as we hunger and thirst for food and drink? How important does it feel to be kept spiritually alive and in good health?
2. How might it affect our behaviour and conversations to be aware that after Communion we are walking out like temples in which Jesus has taken up residence?

All-age talk

(This talk gathers together everyone's response to the Word of God, enabling the different age groups to learn from each other.)

To begin, invite the Rocks to share the Bible verse they have been learning off by heart, and place the words down along the aisle so that people walk over them in order as they come to receive Communion: 'I am the Bread of Life. Whoever comes to me will never be hungry.'

Remind everyone of the way God fed his people in the desert, everyone collecting as much as they needed. The Pebbles have been making some bread (which may now be wafting an appetising smell around the church). And for Communion today we will be using bread which has been specially baked. We'll be receiving a good chunk of it to sense God's feeding, and for those of us who have been fasting, the idea of Jesus feeding the hungry will feel particularly meaningful!

What does it mean for Jesus to be the Bread of Life? Invite the adults to share some of their thinking, and the Boulders to read out the conversation on their sheet. Encourage everyone to come to Communion focusing on the loving way God is feeding us, his children, giving us all the life and spiritual health and strength we need to live out Christian lives of loving service.

Proper 24 – Year B

Sunday between 16 and 22 October inclusive

Called to serve

Thought for the day

Even the Son of Man came not to be served but to serve, and to give his life as a ransom for many.

Reflection on the readings

Job 38:1-7(34-41) or Isaiah 53:4-12
Psalm 104:1-9, 24, 35 or Psalm 91:9-16
Hebrews 5:1-10
Mark 10:35-45

As Christians we are called to serve. The hallmark of our identity as a godly community should be the way all of us go quietly about our lives noticing needs and acting on them; the way we are attentive and available, ready to take part in the boring, the messy and the unglamorous. It should be noticeable that Christians are the ones who enjoy such work whether they are thanked or praised for it or not, and whether they get paid for it or not. Nothing in the way the church is run should look remotely like power-structuring, empire-building or swaggering. For Christians, hierarchy is out, pomposity is out, and loving, humble service is in.

Perhaps that kind of talk gives us the grace at least to blush. We all recognise that there is a great yawning gap between this ideal and the reality. Not only do we see glaring examples in the history of the Church where humble loving service has come last on the list, but we also squirm inwardly at the recognition that our own hearts are far from such natural servanthood. We have far more in common with James and John, keen to be part of the action, but secretly expecting honour from it.

As bread and wine people we need heart transplants. We need servant hearts if we are to be true kingdom people, and there is no way such a heart is detachable. It has to be a permanent fixture, central to our thinking, speaking and doing.

Jesus is the one we follow, and servanthood colours his whole life and being. At every Communion we hear those words: 'This is my body, broken for you', and we commit ourselves to eating the bread and sharing in that brokenness. You cannot get more of a call to servanthood than that. We are to be foot-washers, and in practice that is usually humiliating. I'm not talking about the kind of noble service where our high position as a 'multiple upper doing good to the multiple lowers' allows us to steer clear of real servanthood. I mean the times we are asked to become a 'lower' willingly, by listening instead of pushing our control, not minding that someone else has done the job we usually do, doing an act of kindness when it means being passed over for something we would prefer to be doing – and not resenting that or moaning about it to our friends afterwards.

So often it is the thousands of little incidences which train us, but which we prefer to sidestep. But bread and wine people are a community of loving service, and we all need to work at helping one another grow into servants.

Discussion starters

1. Even if we grasp the idea of being servants, how can we stop ourselves striving to be the most important and highly honoured servants of Christ?
2. Is Jesus' model of servant leadership practical? How can we practise it in our church and in our lives?

Suggested order of service

Things to do and people to do them

The people and the priest:

greet each other in the Lord's name
(this includes an introduction to this teaching Eucharist and any practical details)

confess their sins and are assured of God's forgiveness
(the image of foot-washing is used)

keep silence and pray a Collect

proclaim and respond to the Word of God
- Job 38:1-7 (34-41) or Isaiah 53:4-12 – during the first reading a cross is brought from the back to the front of the church, or an image of the crucifixion from a painting is projected
- Hebrews 5:1-10
- Mark 10:35-45 – the Gospel is read with different voices
- After the Gospel, Pebbles, Rocks, Boulders and adults explore and respond to the Word of God in separate groups, in different parts of the church
- All-age Talk gathers these responses together

pray for the Church and the world
(the Pebbles and Boulders lead this time of prayer)

exchange the Peace

prepare the table
(the Rocks group do this today)

pray the Eucharistic Prayer
(the younger children are gathered round the altar so that they can see)

receive Communion

depart with God's blessing
(everyone is given a reminder of servanthood by the Pebbles as they go)

Time of Confession and Forgiveness

Fill the font with water, and have two people standing beside it, each with a towel.

Invitation to Confession:

'Even the Son of Man did not come to be served, but to serve . . .'

As God's people we have gathered in church this morning. We have come to worship the true and living God who loved our universe into being and is willing to forgive us and wash us clean of all our pride and arrogance. Let us humble ourselves before God, and face up to what we really are, knowing that though God sees it all, it does not stop him loving us, or longing to set us free.

As we sense God looking directly into our eyes and our hearts, let us wash our hands in the water of the font, and receive the cleansing forgiveness which only God can give.

(Play some recorded music as people make their way to the font in silence, wash their hands and have them dried by the servants with towels.)

Old Testament reading

Isaiah 53:4-12

If you have a large wooden cross, have three people carrying it slowly to the front of the church during the reading, and laying it down or setting it up near the altar. Or print an image of the crucifixion – or several paintings – on an acetate and project it on to the wall or a screen during the reading.

Gospel

Mark 10:35-45

A group of readers prepare for reading the Gospel by studying the text and thinking through the subscript, rather as actors would, so that they can act it in the expressions and body language, pauses and so on, as well as the words themselves.

Intercessions

Either gather the Pebbles to their prayer mat and pray with them using symbols of power and servanthood, while everyone else prays, or have the Boulders leading these prayers, with the Pebbles dressed up as symbols of power and servanthood to help everyone focus their prayer.

Some of the Pebbles are wearing crowns, with curtains as robes. They walk round the church (or up and down the centre aisle) as one of the Boulders leads the prayer:

We pray for kings and queens,
presidents, chiefs, mayors and directors,
for all leaders in the Church,
for all managers, MPs, matrons and head teachers,
and for everyone who is in charge and authority.
Lord, make them wise and humble, generous and good.

Other Pebbles wearing aprons or overalls, and carrying brooms and buckets, walk round the church while another person from Boulders leads the prayer:

We pray for all those who clean and cook,
clear up the mess which others leave on the streets,
do the jobs no one thinks are important,
all those who have no power and no rights,
and everyone who is not in charge.
Lord, make them wise and humble, generous and good.

Our Servant King, who came not to be served
but to serve,
and calls us to be loving servants as well,
we pray for each other
and all those we love and look after;
we pray for all those who look after us.
Lord, make us wise and humble, generous and good. Amen.

All-age exploration of the Word PEBBLES

Proper 24 – Year B

Sunday between 16 and 22 October inclusive

Called to serve

Thought for the day

Even the Son of Man came not to be served but to serve, and to give his life as a ransom for many.

Readings

Job 38:1-7(34-41) or Isaiah 53:4-12
Psalm 104:1-9, 24, 35 or Psalm 91:9-16
Hebrews 5:1-10
Mark 10:35-45

Before the service (advance preparation)

- Copy the activity sheets and prepare the area where you will be working.
- Cut some J-cloths or dusters into small (5cm) squares, enough for all the congregation.
- Bring some crowns and curtain 'robes' for some of the group, and aprons, dustpan and brush, mops and buckets for the rest.
- Bring a towel and arrange for one of the group to stand with you by the font at the time of Confession and Forgiveness, drying people's hands.

During the service

- One of the group is drying people's hands during the time of Confession and Forgiveness.
- After the Gospel, gather the group in their work area.

Teaching

Put down a crown and a dustpan and brush, or mop and bucket. First pick up the crown and hold it. Lots of stories have kings in them. What is a king? Someone who is in charge of the land and rules over it. It's the king who gives all the orders, and gets his servants running round after him, doing all the work. (They can practise saying 'Yes, your majesty!' to someone wearing the crown.)

Now pick up the dustpan and brush, or mop and bucket. Servants are the ones who do all the work. They don't get to give orders and they aren't very powerful at all. They are the ones who cook and clean, and do the washing, and tidy up and buy the food, and weed the garden and clean out the gerbils, and put out the rubbish and polish the tables, and scrape mud off the shoes . . . ! (The children can try miming all these as you say them in quick succession, till everyone is out of breath.) Who would they rather be – the king or a servant?

Now Jesus is our King, but he isn't like the kings we've been talking about. Although he's very important and very powerful, he behaves like a servant, looking after people, making them better and cheering them up. He looks after us now, loving us and helping us. (Place the crown on the servant things.)

And Jesus says that if we want to be like him, and follow him, we've got to be like servants as well, not bossing everyone around, but looking out for what they need and being kind and thoughtful.

Explain that there are two servant jobs the Pebbles are doing later in the service. First we are going to help everyone pray today by dressing up as important kings and queens, and then as servants. And at the end of the service we are going to give everyone a tiny duster to remind them that we are all called to be servants. (Show them the pieces of cloth, shared between a few baskets.)

All together

During the All-age Talk the Pebbles will be invited to the front in their aprons/overalls, carrying their dustpans, brushes, mops and buckets. Whoever is giving the All-age Talk will also be referring to the dusters which the Pebbles will be giving out as everyone leaves church.

- The group will be helping Boulders lead the Intercessions by dressing up as those in charge and those not in charge.
- At the end of the service the group stands at the door, giving out miniature cloths and dusters to remind everyone of our calling to humble service.

Notes

Jesus is NOT like this
Jesus IS like this
Colour in
JESUS
the servant King

All-age exploration of the Word ROCKS

Proper 24 – Year B

Sunday between 16 and 22 October inclusive

Called to serve

Thought for the day

Even the Son of Man came not to be served but to serve, and to give his life as a ransom for many.

Readings

Job 38:1-7(34-41) or Isaiah 53:4-12
Psalm 104:1-9, 24, 35 or Psalm 91:9-16
Hebrews 5:1-10
Mark 10:35-45

Before the service (advance preparation)

- Copy the activity sheets and prepare the work area. You will need a cut-out speech bubble with the question on it: 'Can one of us sit at your right hand and the other on your left when you are in glory?'
- Arrange with the president the way the table is going to be prepared for Communion, and ask members of the Rocks group to help with this. They may, for instance, lay the cloth and place on it candles and book during the first hymn, and others bring the bread, wine and water at the offertory. The details will reflect your own church tradition.
- Draw in large bubble letters on several sheets of paper, 'The Son of Man came not to be served but to serve', and invite some of the group to paint the words in. Stick these on the pillars or walls ready for Sunday morning.

During the service

- After the Gospel, gather the group in their work area.

Teaching
First of all everyone reads the question in the speech bubble. They may remember hearing it in the Gospel just now – it was the question which James and John were asking Jesus. Why on earth were they asking it? Because only the most important people would sit on the right and left of the king, and James and John wanted to be the most important people in Jesus' kingdom.

But what kind of a king was Jesus? Take the children round to where they can read the large words on the pillars or walls: 'The Son of Man came not to be served but to serve.' Jesus isn't the kind of king who's into being bossy and throwing his weight around. Use the sheet to look at how Jesus behaves – listening to people no one bothers to listen to, healing those no one bothers to help, noticing the ones most people sneer at. Jesus comes among us as a servant, washing feet – and he says to all his disciples (including us) that he wants us to be like that too. He doesn't want us to be always longing to be really important, or the kind of person everyone admires and is a bit scared of.

He just wants us to be happy servants – the kind of people who notice needs and quietly get on with doing something to help. When the bread is broken and shared at Communion, we remember the way Jesus was willing to give away his whole life in loving service. And when we eat that broken bread, sharing in his life, we are agreeing to do our best to be loving servants as well, because that's what God's kingdom is all about.

All together
Whoever is giving the All-age Talk will be referring to the words on the pillars/walls which some of the Rocks have painted.

- Some of the group will be helping prepare the table for Communion.

Notes

THE SON OF MAN CAME NOT TO BE SERVED BUT TO SERVE

Mark 10:35-45

Write in the words you choose

bossy

listening to people

thoughtful

greedy

wise

kind

fair

strict

proud

strong

cruel

humble

gentle

trampling on people

All-age exploration of the Word
BOULDERS

Proper 24 – Year B

Sunday between 16 and 22 October inclusive

Called to serve

Thought for the day

Even the Son of Man came not to be served but to serve, and to give his life as a ransom for many.

Readings

Job 38:1-7(34-41) or Isaiah 53:4-12
Psalm 104:1-9, 24, 35 or Psalm 91:9-16
Hebrews 5:1-10
Mark 10:35-45

Before the service (advance preparation)

- Copy the sheets and prepare the work area.
- Arrange for two of the group to lead the prayers with the Pebbles, practising so that they give people time to think and pray.
- One or two of the group may like to be involved in the reading of the Gospel.
- If you are using projected images during the first reading from Isaiah, one or two of the group can be in charge of the OHP.

During the service

- Some of the group are taking part in the Gospel reading and leading the Intercessions.
- After the Gospel, gather the group in their work area.

Teaching
Using the reminders on the sheet, think back to the scripture passages we have heard today. If Jesus comes among us as one who serves, and we are called to be the Body of Christ, what would we expect church and church people to be like? They can work in pairs using the sheet to record their ideas, and then as a full group look at how we measure up to this as a church community.

Look together at the foot-washing picture, trying to imagine what it must have been like to be waited on by their master and teacher, wearing a servant's towel. Jesus was acting not like a kingly Messiah, but a low-grade servant! We are reminded of this whenever the bread is broken for us – Jesus shows us what real loving servant work leads to, and invites us to share in the brokenness of the Suffering Servant, through which healing and wholeness can come.

All together
During the All-age Talk the Boulders share some of their ideas about what a serving church would look like.

Notes

SERVANTS NEEDED: ANYONE CAN APPLY

AREN'T SERVANTS THE ONES WHO DO THOSE MESSY JOBS NO ONE ELSE WANTS TO DO?

That's right.

WHY WOULD ANYONE IN THEIR RIGHT MIND CHOOSE TO BE A SERVANT? I'D RATHER BE IN CHARGE AND BOSS EVERYONE AROUND.

Yes, Jesus could have played it that way – after all, God's more powerful than anyone. But he chose the servant role instead.

WHY?

It's all a question of caring love, really. If you love someone, you look out for their needs and help them, instead of bossing them around.

THAT'S A LOT OF LOVING IF YOU'RE TALKING ABOUT EVERYBODY.

Yes, I am. And it is.

All-age exploration of the Word
ADULTS

Proper 24 – Year B

Sunday between 16 and 22 October inclusive

Called to serve

Thought for the day

Even the Son of Man came not to be served but to serve, and to give his life as a ransom for many.

Readings

Job 38:1-7(34-41) or Isaiah 53:4-12
Psalm 104:1-9, 24, 35 or Psalm 91:9-16
Hebrews 5:1-10
Mark 10:35-45

Before the service (advance preparation)

- Copy the sheets and bring a page of flipchart paper and some marker pens.
- Arrange for someone to organise the cross or the projected images for the first reading.
- Arrange for four people (adults and Boulders) to read the Gospel, using a narrator and different parts. (James and John speak together.) They will need to practise together as suggested.
- Ask one of the older members of the church to be one of the servants by the font at the time of Confession and forgiveness. They will be holding a towel and drying people's hands, so that their body language assures people of God's forgiveness.

During the service

- One elderly adult and one young child hold the towels at the font for the time of Confession and Forgiveness.
- Some adults will be involved with the dramatised reading of the Gospel.
- After the Gospel, the adults break into small groups with their enabler.

Teaching
Give out the sheets and invite the group to mention any verses or phrases from today's readings which they particularly love or find moving, or are challenged by. You may find it helpful to read the reflection on the readings now as well. Use the discussion starters to explore and respond to the Word of God, noting down on the flipchart sheet all their thoughts and ideas about the beauty of loving servanthood as well as its demands.

All together
During the all-age talk the adults share their ideas about the beauty of servanthood.

Notes

Called to serve

Thought for the day

Even the Son of Man came not to be served but to serve, and to give his life as a ransom for many.

Reflection on the readings

Job 38:1-7(34-41) or Isaiah 53:4-12
Psalm 104:1-9, 24, 35 or Psalm 91:9-16
Hebrews 5:1-10
Mark 10:35-45

As Christians we are called to serve. The hallmark of our identity as a godly community should be the way all of us go quietly about our lives noticing needs and acting on them; the way we are attentive and available, ready to take part in the boring, the messy and the unglamorous. It should be noticeable that Christians are the ones who enjoy such work whether they are thanked or praised for it or not, and whether they get paid for it or not. Nothing in the way the church is run should look remotely like power-structuring, empire-building or swaggering. For Christians, hierarchy is out, pomposity is out, and loving, humble service is in.

Perhaps that kind of talk gives us the grace at least to blush. We all recognise that there is a great yawning gap between this ideal and the reality. Not only do we see glaring examples in the history of the Church where humble loving service has come last on the list, but we also squirm inwardly at the recognition that our own hearts are far from such natural servanthood. We have far more in common with James and John, keen to be part of the action, but secretly expecting honour from it.

As bread and wine people we need heart transplants. We need servant hearts if we are to be true kingdom people, and there is no way such a heart is detachable – it has to be a permanent fixture, central to our thinking, speaking and doing.

Jesus is the one we follow, and servanthood colours his whole life and being. At every Communion we hear those words: 'This is my body, broken for you', and we commit ourselves to eating the bread and sharing in that brokenness. You cannot get more of a call to servanthood than that. We are to be foot-washers, and in practice that is usually humiliating. I'm not talking about the kind of noble service where our high position as a 'multiple upper doing good to the multiple lowers' allows us to steer clear of real servanthood. I mean the times we are asked to become a 'lower' willingly, by listening instead of pushing our control, not minding that someone else has done the job we usually do, doing an act of kindness when it means being passed over for something we would prefer to be doing – and not resenting that or moaning about it to our friends afterwards.

So often it is the thousands of little incidences which train us, but which we prefer to sidestep. But bread and wine people are a community of loving service, and we all need to work at helping one another grow into servants.

Discussion starters

1. Even if we grasp the idea of being servants, how can we stop ourselves striving to be the most important and highly honoured servants of Christ?
2. Is Jesus' model of servant leadership practical? How can we practise it in our church and in our lives?

All-age talk

(This talk gathers together the responses of the different groups, so that they can all add to each other's experiences and ideas.)

Begin by inviting everyone to look at the words some of the Rocks have decorated for us on the walls, and reading them out together: 'The Son of Man came not to be served but to serve.' Explain that 'Son of Man' is what Jesus often called himself, placing himself alongside us as completely human, having put aside his glory to come and save us. Not surprisingly, Jesus walked about in Palestine behaving like a loving servant, humble and obedient, rather than like some power-happy king.

This means that we, as followers of Jesus, are called to be like servants as well. So what does it mean for us to be a serving community of people? The Boulders share some of their ideas about what a serving church might look like. The adults share their ideas about the beauty of servanthood. The Pebbles gave us a good idea of what it means to serve in the way they dressed up earlier on. Invite some of them up in their aprons/overalls, carrying their dustpans, brushes, mops and buckets.

Point out how they look ready to get started on all those jobs we don't much like doing. Those who serve don't just pick the jobs which get them well appreciated or paid lots of money; they go for whatever jobs need doing, whether they are impressive or not. Those who serve don't just spend time with people they like or want to impress; they give their time and full attention to whoever needs them, whether they are attractive or rather smelly.

Explain that, to help us remember how we are called to be this kind of serving community, the Pebbles group will be giving out small squares of duster cloths to take home with us after church. They are small to remind us that we need to work together as a serving community to be really effective servants. They are dusters to remind us that although God's work is really so important, most people think of loving service as nothing more than weak and time-wasting, since it earns no money.

Loving service is hard, demanding work, and we need to practise it every day, thanking God for the serving opportunities which come our way, rather than resenting them. We cannot share the bread and wine of brokenness and loving servanthood faithfully without putting it straight into action, and committing ourselves once again to the rehabilitating but costly gift of serving others in love and humility.

YEAR C

Third Sunday of Lent – Year C

Strength for the journey

Thought for the day

Regular spiritual feeding gives us the strength to resist temptation and grow in holiness.

Reflection on the readings

Isaiah 55:1-9
Psalm 63:1-8
1 Corinthians 10:1-13
Luke 13:1-9

Junk food is fine now and again but if we try to live entirely on crisps and ice cream we end up weakened and less resistant to disease. Our bodies need regular, wholesome nourishment and clean water to drink if we are to travel healthily through life, and spiritually the same is true. Yet most of us take far less interest in our spiritual diet, and often accept our weakness in the face of temptation with a shrug of the shoulders, assuming it is inevitable, and not realising that our souls need strengthening food for these battles, just as our bodies need strengthening food to equip us to mow the lawn, clean the windows or play a game of football.

Through his prophet, God speaks to his people encouraging them to come and get what God is offering for their spiritual health and strength. Clean water which quenches our deep spiritual thirst is freely available, if only we will take God up on his offer; spiritual feeding which will satisfy our craving hunger is there for free. What is the point of struggling on in our own feeble strength, malnourished and weakened, when the nourishment we need is freely available for the asking?

It isn't that temptation will suddenly disappear if we are feeding regularly at the table of the Lord, any more than eating regular healthy meals means the windows no longer need cleaning. We are not promised immunity from temptation. As Paul points out in the letter to the Corinthians, the people of Israel were all drinking from the rock, but many of them still fell into sin when they were tempted.

The big difference is that we are now provided with the strength for the job, if we choose to call on it. Think of those emergencies when physically we summon every scrap of strength and energy to get us out of a dangerous position. That is the image we need to keep in mind with regard to our battles with temptation. We need both the good, regular healthy feeding of Christ, and the determination to call on those resources when we are tempted, using them to the full. That way we are working 'yoked up' to Jesus, still there in the battle zone, but no longer on our own, or poorly equipped. With Christ's strength we can fight and win.

Discussion starters

1. Have you been consciously receiving the bread and wine at Communion as power food which equips you and strengthens you spiritually for battle? If not, how might this change your approach to Communion?
2. Share with the group any tips you have found helpful and effective in fighting temptation – the more we can encourage one another in this, the stronger bread and wine people we shall be.

Suggested order of service

Things to do and people to do them

The people and the priest:

greet each other in the Lord's name
(this includes an introduction to the teaching Eucharist and any practical details)

confess their sins and are assured of God's forgiveness
(today this focuses on the way we have given in to temptation)

keep silence and pray a Collect

proclaim and respond to the Word of God

- Isaiah 55:1-9 – this reading is spoken in the context of a street vendor
- 1 Corinthians 10:1-13 – this passage has an accompanying action
- Luke 13:1-9 – the second part of the Gospel is acted out
- After the Gospel, Pebbles, Rocks, Boulders and adults respond to the Word in their own teaching, in different parts of the church
- All-age talk gathers these responses together

pray for the Church and the world
(using the whole building as a holy space)

exchange the Peace

prepare the table
(the Boulders group help with this)

pray the Eucharistic Prayer
(the younger children are gathered around the altar so that they can see what is going on)

receive Communion

depart with God's blessing

Time of Confession and Forgiveness

Invite everyone to remember the times they have been tempted, and in their own strength have been too weak to stop themselves falling into sin. Have some recorded music playing quietly as people are given the space to bring these occasions to mind in penitence.

> Empowering God,
> we confess that we have failed to hold fast to you
> in times of testing,
> and in that weakness we have fallen into
> temptation.
> We are very sorry, and repent of our sin.

The words of forgiveness are proclaimed.

Old Testament reading

Isaiah 55:1-9

The reader starts at the back of the church and shouts the first two verses as s/he walks up to the front, carrying a picnic hamper or cool box, and a large water container with cup attached. When they reach the front they pour out some water and drink a few sips before continuing with verse 3. They hold the water and sip from it from time to time as the rest of the passage is read, coaxing the people to try this godly life as a street vendor might encourage us to try a product. The water, cup and hamper are left near the altar to remind people of God's offer as they come to receive the bread and wine at Communion.

New Testament reading

1 Corinthians 10:1-13

Just before the passage is read, someone does a balancing act, such as standing on a wobble board or standing in a one-legged position. The president draws attention to the way they have to concentrate hard to avoid falling, which is what Paul is talking about in this letter to the Corinthians. Whether you are reading the whole passage or just verses 12-13, the balancing continues throughout as people listen to the words.

Gospel

Luke 13:1-9

At verse 6 a gardener with his spade pretends to be digging and the garden owner walks up to the front, looking at various plants and examining them, till he joins the gardener at the front and examines his fig tree. He says verse 7 either learnt by heart or using his own words, and the gardener, obviously fond of the tree, replies in the same way.

Intercessions

As recorded music plays, people move around the building on a prayer trail, using it as a metaphor to help their prayer focus. At the different parts of the building they can pray in the words provided or in their own words. Here are some suggested points of prayer, though your own trail will naturally use your own building. People walk around in pairs or threes, adults with children, older children with younger ones, so that all are involved at their own level.

- *At a clear window:*
  Pray for the light of God's wisdom to make things clear to those who are confused or doubtful.
- *At a stained glass window:*
  Thank God for colour and light in our lives, and ask for the church to be full of Christians who let God's light shine through them.
- *At a main door:*
  Pray for all who come and go here. Pray for those who are new to the faith, and those who have stopped believing. Pray for those who feel shut out of life.
- *At the altar or holy table:*
  Thank God for his strengthening food and pray for the Holy Spirit to fill us with love like Jesus' costly love.
- *At the lectern:*
  Pray that the Word of God may take root in our lives so that we grow up strongly in Christ, bearing fruit.
- *At the pews:*
  Pray for the world, and our calling to go out in the power of the Spirit, bringing God's healing and love.

All-age exploration of the Word PEBBLES

Third Sunday of Lent – Year C

Strength for the journey

Thought for the day

Regular spiritual feeding gives us the strength to resist temptation and grow in holiness.

Readings

Isaiah 55:1-9
Psalm 63:1-8
1 Corinthians 10:1-13
Luke 13:1-9

Before the service (advance preparation)

- Copy the activity sheets and prepare the work area. You will need a jug of water and some plastic cups, scissors, crayons and glue.

During the service

- After the Gospel, gather the group in their work area.

Teaching
Place the jug and cups down in the centre of the group and remind them of the person who was drinking during the reading from Isaiah. Give the children a drink of water, and talk about how good it is to drink when we are really thirsty.

God invites us to come to him and drink a different kind of water. It isn't just our bodies which get thirsty and need a drink. Our souls, which live for ever, need spiritual food and drink as well. We get that from spending time with God, talking and listening to him in prayer, reading the Bible and coming to church with our Christian brothers and sisters to worship God and meet him in Communion.

Help them make their sheet into a cup to drink out of.

All together
During the All-age Talk the Pebbles will show the cups they have made, and remind everyone of how God invites us to drink his water of life.

Notes

HOW TO MAKE A PAPER CUP

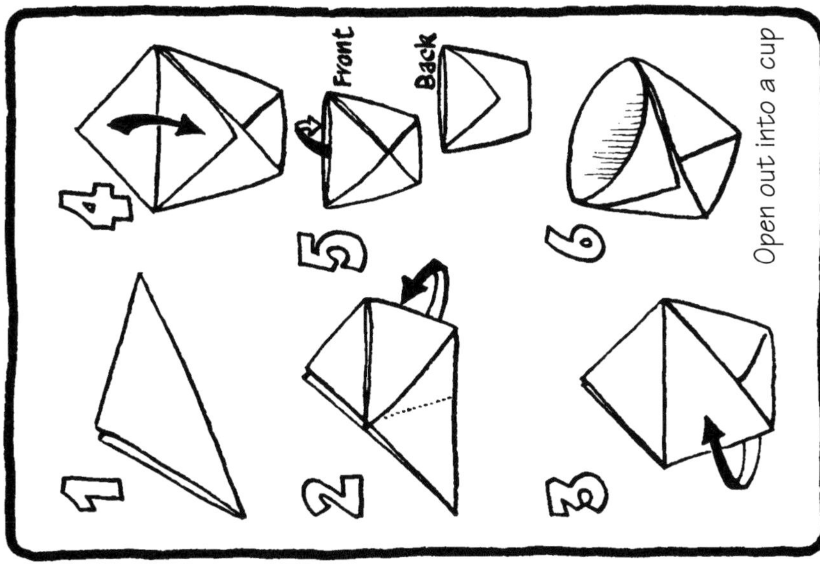

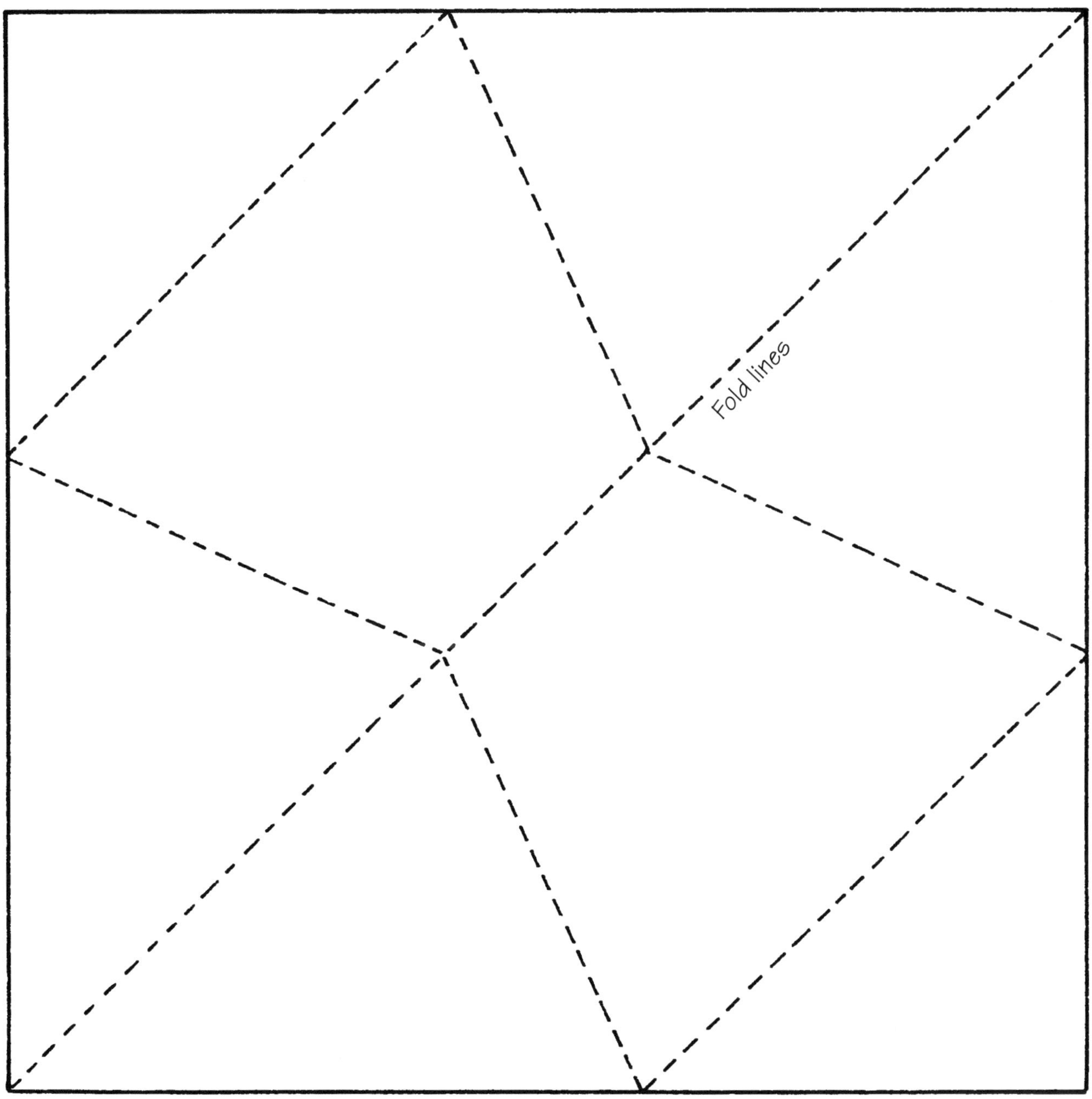

All-age exploration of the Word
ROCKS

Third Sunday of Lent – Year C

Strength for the journey

Thought for the day

Regular spiritual feeding gives us the strength to resist temptation and grow in holiness.

Readings

Isaiah 55:1-9
Psalm 63:1-8
1 Corinthians 10:1-13
Luke 13:1-9

Before the service (advance preparation)

- Copy the activity sheets and prepare the work area. Bring a pot plant which is not thriving very well, a bigger pot, some more earth and some water.
- Cut some blue and green lengths of crêpe paper for the Rocks to wave during some of the hymns.

During the service

- After the Gospel, gather the group in their work area.

Teaching
Place down the pot plant and remind them of the Gospel, with the gardener and the fig tree. The gardener didn't want the tree to be thrown out until he had given it lots of good nourishing food and water to help it grow strong. Talk over with them what you could do with your pot plant to help it grow better, and let them help you give this plant what it needs.

When it is looking happier in its new pot, talk about the way we need feeding too, not just our bodies but our souls as well. When we come to Communion, Jesus is feeding us spiritual food and drink, to make us strong and healthy, and resistant to evil. We need that feeding or we get weak and can't fight off the dragons of temptation! God has the supplies of strength we need to stand up for what is right and good and honest and fair. It doesn't cost anything to get them, either – God offers them to us for free.*

As we share the bread and wine at Communion or receive God's blessing there at the altar, what happens is that invisibly our souls are being fed all the power and goodness they need to make us strong in the battle.

All together
During the all-age talk the Rocks will share some of their ideas about God's invisible feeding.

- At the offertory and dismissal hymns the children wave their streamers.

Notes

* The idea of fighting off evil needs to be handled with sensitivity. It certainly is a battle and we need to prepare children for this, but we are not encouraging them to use violence as a way of solving problems. I have deliberately chosen the dragon image to place the battle in the land of story, so they can understand it as a symbol. Stress the real weapons against evil as courage, prayer, truth, hope and God's power of love.

As we SHARE the BREAD and WINE invisibly our SOULS are being FED all the POWER and GOODNESS they need to make us STRONG in the BATTLE against EVIL
GOD'S POWER
HOPE
Take whatever you need.
strength COURAGE
strength PRAYER
strength TRUTH
Draw you fighting the dragon of evil and temptation!

All-age exploration of the Word
BOULDERS

Third Sunday of Lent – Year C

Strength for the journey

Thought for the day

Regular spiritual feeding gives us the strength to resist temptation and grow in holiness.

Readings

Isaiah 55:1-9
Psalm 63:1-8
1 Corinthians 10:1-13
Luke 13:1-9

Before the service (advance preparation)

- Copy the sheets and prepare the area where you will be working.
- One of the Boulders group who likes acting may like to be the reader of the Isaiah passage or involved in the acting of the Gospel.
- Arrange with the president for the Boulders group to prepare the table for Communion during the service.

During the service

- Some of the group may be involved with the readings.
- After the Gospel, gather the group in their work area.

Teaching
Two of the group can read the factfile which introduces the teaching on coping with temptation as a scripted conversation. Read again verses 12 and 13 of 1 Corinthians 10, linking this with the cartoon on the sheet and talking together about ways they have found useful in dealing with temptation (such as walking away from trouble, seeing the funny side to diffuse an explosive situation, doing something positive when you're feeling destructive and so on). They can record helpful ideas on the sheet for future use.

Now look at the idea of spiritual feeding to empower us and strengthen us to resist temptation. God's feeding at Communion is invisible – Jesus comes to us hidden in the act of eating bread and drinking wine together, but the power of that risen life living in our own lives is very real and effective. All we have to do is trust it and use it.

It won't take us out of the temptation but will equip us with the strength to resist and win over evil. We might think we just happen to be weaker than anyone else so it's OK for us to lack self-control; we use weakness as an excuse for falling into sin. But the truth is that on our own we are all weak, and in God's strength we can all be strong.

As you discuss these things, aim to create a climate where the young people feel safe enough to raise difficult questions and face uncomfortable areas, so they are enabled to grow in faith.

All together
During the All-age Talk, two Boulders will read the conversation about temptation.

- Several of the group help prepare the table for Communion.

Notes

COPING WITH TEMPTATION

I COULD COPE WITH OTHER PEOPLE'S TEMPTATIONS – IT'S MY OWN THAT ARE SO HARD TO RESIST.

Yes, temptations always push at us where we're most weak or vulnerable.

DOES THAT MEAN WE HAVE AN EXCUSE FOR GIVING IN TO THEM?

It's a good reason but not an excuse, because it *is* possible to stand firm and resist temptation.

HOW?

If we stick really close to God he may not take away the temptation, but he *will* give us the strength we need. It's still a difficult battle but in God's strength we can win.

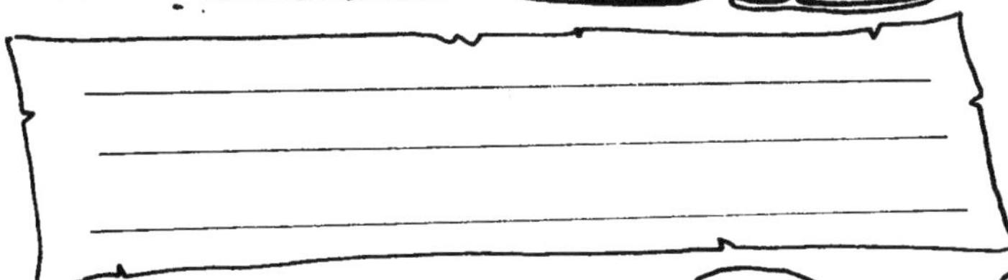

All-age exploration of the Word
ADULTS

Third Sunday of Lent – Year C

Strength for the journey

Thought for the day

Regular spiritual feeding gives us the strength to resist temptation and grow in holiness.

Readings

Isaiah 55:1-9
Psalm 63:1-8
1 Corinthians 10:1-13
Luke 13:1-9

Before the service (advance preparation)

- Copy the sheets and prepare a page of flipchart paper headed: 'Lead us not into temptation but deliver us from evil.' You will also need marker pens or crayons.
- Three adults/Boulders are needed for the Gospel – one to read and the others to mime.
- An adult or a Boulder who is comfortable acting is needed for the Isaiah reading.
- Someone is needed to balance in a one-legged position just before the reading from 1 Corinthians 10 and during verses 12-13 of it.

During the service

- Some people will be involved in the readings.
- After the Gospel, the adults split into small groups, each with an enabler.

Teaching
Read the Thought for the Day, and talk over the readings, sharing anything which has suddenly made sense or which is hard to understand. It may be helpful for people to read the reflection on the readings before using the discussion starters to help you tackle the problems of temptation! Keep a note of thoughts and ideas on the large sheet, or invite everyone in the group to write a few words or draw a symbol to express what they feel God is teaching us today.

All together
During the All-age Talk the adults will share some of their thoughts on the spiritual feeding we receive at Communion.

Notes

Strength for the journey

Thought for the day

Regular spiritual feeding gives us the strength to resist temptation and grow in holiness.

Reflection on the readings

Isaiah 55:1-9
Psalm 63:1-8
1 Corinthians 10:1-13
Luke 13:1-9

Junk food is fine now and again but if we try to live entirely on crisps and ice cream we end up weakened and less resistant to disease. Our bodies need regular, wholesome nourishment and clean water to drink if we are to travel healthily through life, and spiritually the same is true. Yet most of us take far less interest in our spiritual diet, and often accept our weakness in the face of temptation with a shrug of the shoulders, assuming it is inevitable, and not realising that our souls need strengthening food for these battles, just as our bodies need strengthening food to equip us to mow the lawn, clean the windows or play a game of football.

Through his prophet, God speaks to his people encouraging them to come and get what God is offering for their spiritual health and strength. Clean water which quenches our deep spiritual thirst is freely available, if only we will take God up on his offer; spiritual feeding which will satisfy our craving hunger is there for free. What is the point of struggling on in our own feeble strength, malnourished and weakened, when the nourishment we need is freely available for the asking?

It isn't that temptation will suddenly disappear if we are feeding regularly at the table of the Lord, any more than eating regular healthy meals means the windows no longer need cleaning. We are not promised immunity from temptation. As Paul points out in the letter to the Corinthians, the people of Israel were all drinking from the rock, but many of them still fell into sin when they were tempted.

The big difference is that we are now provided with the strength for the job, if we choose to call on it. Think of those emergencies when physically we summon every scrap of strength and energy to get us out of a dangerous position. That is the image we need to keep in mind with regard to our battles with temptation. We need both the good, regular healthy feeding of Christ, and the determination to call on those resources when we are tempted, using them to the full. That way we are working 'yoked up' to Jesus, still there in the battle zone, but no longer on our own, or poorly equipped. With Christ's strength we can fight and win.

Discussion starters

1. Have you been consciously receiving the bread and wine at Communion as power food which equips you and strengthens you spiritually for battle? If not, how might this change your approach to Communion?
2. Share with the group any tips you have found helpful and effective in fighting temptation – the more we can encourage one another in this, the stronger bread and wine people we shall be.

All-age talk

(This talk gathers the different groups' responses to the Word of God, enabling us all to learn from one another.)

Start by inviting the Pebbles to show the cups they have made, and remind everyone of how God invites us to drink deeply from the refreshing and cleansing water of his life, just as the passage from Isaiah encouraged us to do in the first reading we heard this morning.

Now ask two of the Boulders to read their scripted conversation about temptation. We all find temptation hard to resist, whatever age we are, and however long or short a time we have been a Christian. The bad news is that temptation doesn't get any easier as you get older or more holy – in fact, the saints seem to have massive battles against evil to deal with, the holier they get!

But there is good news as well, and it's very good news. We come into God's presence and he feeds us with the strength and power we need to resist evil and fight temptation. That strength is the life of Jesus, living in us as we live in him, and it is extremely effective – as long as we use it! We could jump out of a plane at 10,000 feet with the best and most reliable parachute in the world, but if we don't pull the cord to open it up, we'll still end up crashing to the ground in rather a hurry.

So how can we make sure we remember to use the feeding we are getting week by week as bread and wine people? How can we be a community really energised and strengthened by the spiritual food we are so lovingly provided with?

Ask the adult group leaders to show the ideas their groups have come up with, and invite the Rocks to share their ideas as well. Thank everyone, and encourage the whole congregation not just to spend time in church together on a Sunday, but to support each other in prayer during the week as well, and to pray for one another as we all walk up to Communion. That way we shall be fed not just as individuals, but as a whole community of faith, and God will be able to use us for a force of great good in this place where we live.

Fifth Sunday of Easter – Year C

Living by love and forgiveness

Thought for the day

We are called to be a people so full of Christ's life that we live by love and forgiveness.

Reflection on the readings

Acts 11:1-18
Psalm 148
Revelation 21:1-6
John 13:31-35

In the early days of the Church, when it was seen by the Roman authorities as a subversive cult, half-heard rumours accused Christians of cannibalism, because they talked about eating bread and drinking wine as the body and blood of Christ. Clearly it isn't cannibalism which we are about, but we are instructed by Jesus to eat and drink as signs that we are taking into ourselves the life force of another person. Not just any person but the human person who is also God – Jesus himself. That is a serious and challenging command, and one we do well to rethink regularly in order to grasp the enormity of what is going on at Communion.

Today's Gospel helps us make some sense of it. The new commandment Jesus gives his disciples is to love one another in exactly the way Jesus loves them. How do we begin to obey such a daunting command?

If we try simply imitating Jesus, we can end up by copying some of the behaviour, but love is a slippery thing which can't be copied without losing its essence; love has to be the genuine article or it stops being love. Something more drastic is needed than the copycat model. What we need is somehow to possess the genuine essence of Jesus' loving as part of our very being, so that the way we then perceive and respond to others resonates authentically with the actual love of Christ.

And that is exactly what happens when we gather to recall Jesus' life-giving love on the cross, and eat the sign of his costly brokenness. There is no way we can share in Christ's love and remain unbroken ourselves. Such love means accepting vulnerability and heartache, and rejecting the comforts of insulated living. The moment of receiving Communion is one when at one level we may well feel very exposed indeed, because to accept living in tandem with the living God, our hearts fused with his loving, is to be out in the windswept wastes of need, bearing in our bodies the precious brokenness which only heals through self-giving. Bread sharers become Christ bearers.

Discussion starters

1. Are we prepared for the cost of discipleship, or do we half-expect Jesus to come up with a discount deal for us, where we won't actually have to involve ourselves in such wholesale loving and forgiving?
2. How does the kind of love which is willing to be broken become a force for great healing?

Suggested order of service

Things to do and people to do them

The people and the priest:

greet each other in the Lord's name
(this includes an introduction to this teaching Eucharist and any practical details)

confess their sins and are assured of God's forgiveness
(which focuses today on our resistance to God's transforming)

keep silence and pray a Collect

proclaim and respond to the Word of God

- Acts 11:1-18 – this passage is read communally
- Revelation 21:1-6
- John 13:31-35 – the Gospel is accompanied by recorded music
- After the Gospel, Pebbles, Rocks, Boulders and adults respond to the Word in their own teaching, in different parts of the church
- All-age Talk gathers these responses together

pray for the Church and the world
(this time of prayer is led by representatives of different age groups)

exchange the Peace

prepare the table
(representatives of different church organisations help with this)

pray the Eucharistic Prayer
(the younger children are gathered around the altar so that they can see)

receive Communion

depart with God's blessing

Time of Confession and Forgiveness

As an introduction to the Confession you may like to use this short meditation.

Invite everyone to think of their life as a house, and walk round it in their mind's eye with Jesus – the rooms you are ashamed of, as well as the more public rooms you have carefully put in order. Look in the 'grudge cupboards' to see if there are any lurking grudges or old bits of resentment in there; Jesus will help you sweep them out. Look in the 'cravings drawer' and clear it out; take the wrappings off any gifts you are trying to keep intact instead of using; find the key to the inner room you like to keep all to yourself, and let Jesus in.

New Testament reading

Acts 11:1-18

This can be read communally, using pew Bibles or printing the passage out. Everyone reads the words of the Jerusalem 'circumcise the Gentiles' group in verses 3 and 18. Other voices are needed for Peter, the voice speaking to Peter (in verses 7-9) and the angel speaking to Cornelius (in verse 13) and Jesus' voice in verse 16.

Gospel

John 13:31-35

As the Gospel is read, play some quiet, recorded music which fades in at verse 32 and continues a short while after the end of the reading, before the reader announces the end.

Intercessions

Representatives of different age groups lead the time of prayer, like this:

Let us pray as the Body of Christ
for the Church and for the world,
bearing in mind that the mark of Jesus' friends
is their love for one another.

(A woman)
All of us who are adults want to thank God
for the children and young people
and pray for them now.

Heavenly Father,
bless the children and young people
growing up in our church community
and all over the world.
Keep them safe
and help them to grow strong in faith and love.

Silence

(A boy)
All of us who are children and young people
thank God for the grown-ups
and pray for them now.

Heavenly Father,
bless all the grown-ups in our church community
and all over the world.
Keep them close to you each day,
and guide them to think, speak and do
what makes you happy.

Silence

(A man)
All of us who are men or boys
thank God for the women and girls
of this community and all over the world,
and pray for them now.

Heavenly Father,
we commend to your love and guidance
all daughters, sisters, mothers and wives.
We pray especially for any who are oppressed
or heavily burdened.

Silence

(A girl)
All of us who are girls or women
thank God for the men and boys
of this community and all over the world,
and pray for them now.

Heavenly Father,
we commend to your love and guidance
all sons, brothers, fathers and husbands.
We pray especially for any who are oppressed
or heavily burdened.

(All)
As a church, may our light so shine before others
that they may see our good works
and glorify our Father who is in heaven. Amen.

Preparing the table

One adult, one young person and one child help prepare the table, laying the cloth and placing candles and so on during the first hymn, and bringing the bread, wine and water at the offertory.

All-age exploration of the Word
PEBBLES

Fifth Sunday of Easter – Year C

Living by love and forgiveness

Thought for the day

We are called to be a people so full of Christ's life that we live by love and forgiveness.

Readings

Acts 11:1-18
Psalm 148
Revelation 21:1-6
John 13:31-35

Before the service (advance preparation)

- Copy the activity sheets and prepare the area where you will be working.
- Bring a long sheet of lining paper and plenty of crayons, so that during the readings the children can draw their ideas of people showing God's love in the world.

During the service

- After the Gospel, gather the group in their work area.

Teaching

Have everyone sitting around the drawings, and talk about them together, celebrating all the kind and loving things which go on in our world. (Bad news is only news because it's still quite unusual!)

Where does all that loving come from? It comes from God. God is the only place love can come from because God is completely loving in every way. He pours out his love into the whole universe, and sometimes people realise what's happening and thank him, and sometimes they don't. But God goes on with the loving just the same.

Draw a sun on the lining paper. It's God's love which made our universe and keeps it going. Draw a person. God's love made people, and each one of us.

Show all their drawings again. God loves us very much, and he wants us to love other people like that, sharing, being kind to one another, listening and laughing and crying together, being thoughtful and helping one another, praying for one another, comforting one another, and lots of other caring, brave and good things.

Draw two friends playing, and talk with the children about what they like playing with their friends. Jesus says that whenever we are loving, we are his special friends.

Help them turn their sheets into an 'I am a friend of Jesus' hat, which is worn to remind them to live like Jesus' friends.

All together

The hats the Pebbles have been making are given to them during the All-age Talk, to show that when we love as Jesus loves us, people will know us as Jesus' friends.

Notes

Stick A to B and C to D.
Adjust to fit.

Cut here

All-age exploration of the Word
ROCKS

Fifth Sunday of Easter – Year C

Living by love and forgiveness

Thought for the day

We are called to be a people so full of Christ's life that we live by love and forgiveness.

Readings

Acts 11:1-18
Psalm 148
Revelation 21:1-6
John 13:31-35

Before the service (advance preparation)

- Copy the sheets and prepare the area where you will be working. You will also need to bring a bread roll and a plate.
- Arrange for a boy and a girl to help lead the Intercessions, together with a man and a woman.
- Arrange for one of the group to help prepare the table.

During the service

- After the Gospel, gather the group in the work area.

Teaching
Empty your purse or wallet of its money and credit cards, and work out together a few of the things you could get with all this wealth. Whenever we want to buy something we have to look at what it costs and whether we can afford it. If it's too costly we may either decide not to get it, or, if it seems really important, we might go without something else for a while to pay for it.

Being a Christian is very expensive, though not necessarily with money. (Gather up the money and put it away. Replace it with a cross or crucifix.) Remind everyone of what we heard in the Gospel – Jesus gave his disciples a new command: to love one another in the way Jesus loved them. How did Jesus love them? (They can follow the different strands on the sheet to find out.) Just when he felt like it? No! Just until it started to get him into danger? No! By trying to control their lives for them? No! Loving and forgiving them, through the best and the worst times? Yes!

We only have to look at the cross or crucifix (look at one in church) to see the cost of this kind of loving – it cost Jesus his whole life, and he still reckoned it was worth it. He loves us enough to give up his life for us. And now let's look at that new command again: 'Love one another *as I have loved you.*' That means we're being told to love one another the expensive way – putting ourselves out for one another, going on loving whether it's easy or hard work, loving when we'd rather just please ourselves, and loving even when that means giving up wanting our own way.

Place a bread roll on a plate and explain that this kind of expensive loving is what Jesus was talking about when he broke the bread (break it) and said it was like his own life being broken and given up so that we could be set free from evil and sin. When we share in the consecrated bread at Communion we are being invited to share in the expensive way of loving, and at the same time being invisibly fed with the strength to do it.

All together
During the All-age Talk the Rocks will share what loving like Jesus *doesn't* mean.

- Some of the children will be involved in the Intercessions and the preparing of the table.

Notes

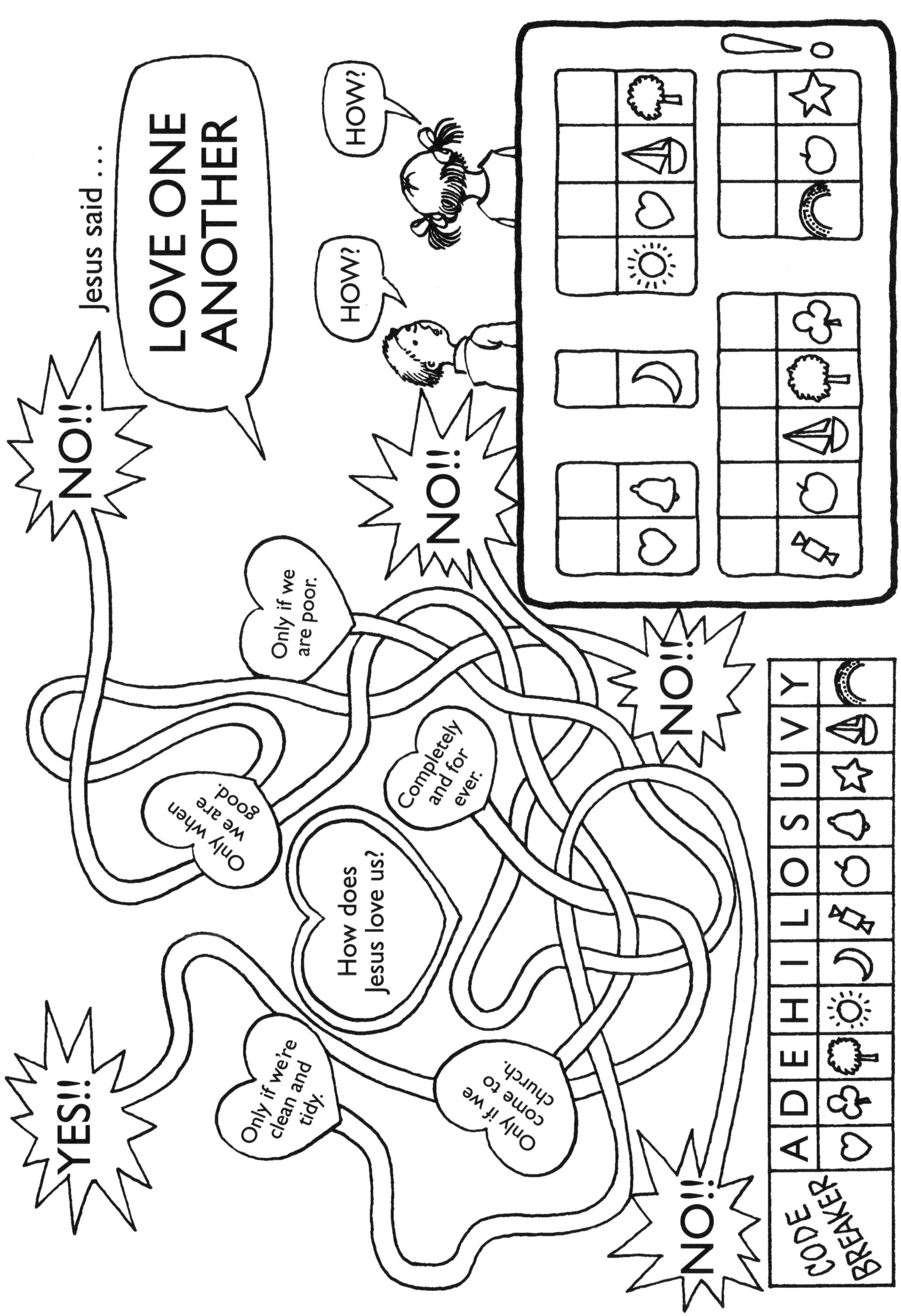
Jesus said . . .
LOVE ONE ANOTHER
HOW?
HOW?
NO!!
NO!!
NO!!
NO!!
YES!!
Only if we are poor.
Only when we are good.
Completely and for ever.
How does Jesus love us?
Only if we're clean and tidy.
Only if we come to church.
CODE BREAKER
A D E H I L O S U V Y

All-age exploration of the Word
BOULDERS

Fifth Sunday of Easter – Year C

Living by love and forgiveness

Thought for the day

We are called to be a people so full of Christ's life that we live by love and forgiveness.

Readings

Acts 11:1-18
Psalm 148
Revelation 21:1-6
John 13:31-35

Before the service (advance preparation)

- Copy the sheets and prepare the area where you will be working. Collect a number of books from the library or local Christian bookshop which tell the story of Christians facing danger or hardship for the love of one another. You will also need to bring a bread roll.
- Some of the group may be involved in practising for the first reading.
- One or two of the group may be organising the background music with the reader of the Gospel.

During the service

- Some may be reading, acting or in charge of the background music.
- After the Gospel, gather the group in their work area.

Teaching
On the sheet there are scripts of people involved in the kind of expensive loving which Jesus told us to do – loving one another in the way he loves us. Have different members of the group reading these out and using the chart on the sheet to identify areas of sacrificial loving in the examples. Introduce the books you have collected, and lend them out for further reading.

It's one thing to be told to do this kind of loving, and another to have the will, strength and heart to do it! How does it happen? Are all these people superhuman, or a different species from most of us?

Hold the bread roll as you talk about the way we need to be fed with the will, heart and strength we need to love as Jesus loves us. We need feeding with nothing less than the loving life of Jesus himself. And that's what happens at Communion, when we hear those words spoken over the bread: 'Take, eat, this is my body, which is given for you. Do this in remembrance of me.' To feed us the bread has to be broken. (Break the bread.) To feed us with his life, Jesus' life has to be broken. And by feeding on him in our hearts by faith with thanksgiving, we shall grow so strong in his love that we *are* able to love with that costly kind of loving.

All together
During the All-age Talk the Boulders will show their broken bread.

- One representative helps prepare the table for Communion.

Notes

SACRIFICIAL LOVING	1	2	3
INVOLVING MONEY			
INVOLVING TIME			
INVOLVING PERSEVERANCE			

THE SCHOOL OF LOVING

I'VE NEVER HEARD OF THAT SCHOOL. CAN ANYONE GO TO IT?

You already do, as a matter of fact. It's called LIFE.

YOU MEAN THE REASON WE'RE ALL HERE IS TO LEARN HOW TO LOVE?

That's about it. Loving and forgiving take quite a bit of learning. At least a lifetime.

DOES THAT MEAN THAT THE OLDER YOU ARE, THE BETTER YOU GET?

Not necessarily. But the deeper our friendship with Jesus becomes, the more loving we'll get. And that's a promise.

All-age exploration of the Word
ADULTS

Fifth Sunday of Easter – Year C
Living by love and forgiveness

Thought for the day

We are called to be a people so full of Christ's life that we live by love and forgiveness.

Readings

Acts 11:1-18
Psalm 148
Revelation 21:1-6
John 13:31-35

Before the service (advance preparation)

- Copy the sheets and prepare a large heart-shaped sheet of paper.
- Some people will be practising for the first reading, with someone taking responsibility for making the text available for the whole congregation.
- One man and one woman will need to take responsibility for leading the Intercessions, together with a boy and a girl from the Rocks group.
- One person prepares the meditation to introduce the time of Confession and Forgiveness.
- One adult representative helps prepare the table for Communion during the service.

During the service

- Different adults will be involved in the readings, the time of Confession, the Intercessions and the preparation of the table for Communion.
- After the Gospel, the adults break into small groups all over the church, each with an enabler.

Teaching

Remind one another of the readings, sharing any insights, challenges or questions raised by them. Read the reflection on the readings before using the discussion starters. On the heart-shaped paper keep track of the thoughts and ideas about the costly love of Jesus, and its implications for us in our own lives.

All together

During the All-age Talk the adults will share their ideas about loving like Jesus.

Notes

Living by love and forgiveness

Thought for the day

We are called to be a people so full of Christ's life that we live by love and forgiveness.

Reflection on the readings

Acts 11:1-18
Psalm 148
Revelation 21:1-6
John 13:31-35

In the early days of the Church, when it was seen by the Roman authorities as a subversive cult, half-heard rumours accused Christians of cannibalism, because they talked about eating bread and drinking wine as the body and blood of Christ. Clearly it isn't cannibalism which we are about, but we are instructed by Jesus to eat and drink as signs that we are taking into ourselves the life force of another person. Not just any person but the human person who is also God – Jesus himself. That is a serious and challenging command, and one we do well to rethink regularly in order to grasp the enormity of what is going on at Communion.

Today's Gospel helps us make some sense of it. The new commandment Jesus gives his disciples is to love one another in exactly the way Jesus loves them. How do we begin to obey such a daunting command?

If we try simply imitating Jesus, we can end up by copying some of the behaviour, but love is a slippery thing which can't be copied without losing its essence; love has to be the genuine article or it stops being love. Something more drastic is needed than the copycat model. What we need is somehow to possess the genuine essence of Jesus' loving as part of our very being, so that the way we then perceive and respond to others resonates authentically with the actual love of Christ.

And that is exactly what happens when we gather to recall Jesus' life-giving love on the cross, and eat the sign of his costly brokenness. There is no way we can share in Christ's love and remain unbroken ourselves. Such love means accepting vulnerability and heartache, and rejecting the comforts of insulated living. The moment of receiving Communion is one when at one level we may well feel very exposed indeed, because to accept living in tandem with the living God, our hearts fused with his loving, is to be out in the windswept wastes of need, bearing in our bodies the precious brokenness which only heals through self-giving. Bread sharers become Christ bearers.

Discussion starters

1. Are we prepared for the cost of discipleship, or do we half-expect Jesus to come up with a discount deal for us, where we won't actually have to involve ourselves in such wholesale loving and forgiving?
2. How does the kind of love which is willing to be broken become a force for great healing?

All-age talk

(Everyone in church has been breaking open the Word of God and this talk enables people to learn from one another and share insights and learning.)

Bring along a huge heart-shaped piece of red paper or fabric and a large cut-out question mark. First show the heart as you refer to the love we have all been thinking about this morning – to be bread and wine people is to be a community of love. But what does that mean? (Place the question mark over the heart.) Invite the Rocks to share with everyone what they've discovered it *doesn't* mean. (They all read out 'How does Jesus love us?' Then one by one they ask the questions, and the whole group shouts each 'No!') Now invite them to share with us what they discovered it *does* mean. (One reads the question and all shout, 'Yes!')

Remind everyone of the end of today's Gospel – that it is through seeing us loving as Jesus loves us that people will know we are Jesus' friends, and the Pebbles have been making hats to help them remember that. (Give out the hats to those in the Pebbles group, encouraging everyone else to imagine they are wearing an invisible hat like this all the time, wherever they go and whomever they talk to. We can all use our hats – real, imagined or invisible – to check that our thoughts, words and actions are indeed loving.

As we all know, real loving is not a comfortable, cosy way for us to live, any more than the cross was a comfortable place for Jesus. Invite the Boulders to show their broken bread. If bread is going to be food, it can't stay complete and unbroken. It has to be broken so that it can be shared and eaten as food. Invite some of the adults to share what they have learnt about loving with Jesus' love, and the way he has linked the command to do it with equipping us to do it. Later on in the Eucharist the priest will say the words of Jesus over the bread and wine, and it will be like all of us being there at the Last Supper with those first disciples, being told by Jesus to love one another as he has loved us, and being fed with Jesus' loving life so that we are equipped to go out of church and start doing just that.

Proper 8 – Year C

Sunday between 26 June and 2 July inclusive

Freed to serve

Thought for the day

Get rid of the old, imprisoning regime and let the new life of loving service liberate you to bear good fruit.

Reflection on the readings

2 Kings 2:1-2, 6-14 or 1 Kings 19:15-16, 19-21
Psalm 77:1-2, 11-20 or Psalm 16
Galatians 5:1, 13-25
Luke 9:51-62

What does it mean for us to be 'bread and wine people'? Are we a religious club? Illusioned comfort-cravers? Morality activists? Reality refusers? Historical costume freaks? Or what? Perhaps we must shamefacedly admit that we are indeed all these here and there and from time to time, just as we are so often perceived and portrayed. But we know equally well that these models are nothing like our calling, or what the Church at its most authentic can be.

Today's readings give us some idea of what we are really called to be, and we need courage to read them candidly because they make uncomfortable and challenging reading. If, as followers of Christ, we have indeed allowed our sin-directed nature to be crucified, shouldn't the results show?

We should expect to find in this community of Christ-followers young, tender shoots and healthy maturing trees, vigorous fruiting and strong root systems. We might expect to find ourselves violently disliked and disapproved of by the worldly for our refusal as a community to comply with corruption and injustice, and for ruffling feathers wherever oppression rules and validity is sidelined.

At the same time we might expect to find a regular flow of enquirers drawn to this vibrant, alternative community, fascinated by the way we are able to live in love, even where there is strong disagreement, and by the unusually simple, uncomplicated way we warmly respond to needs without complex sub-agendas, and by the infectious, good-natured fun and open friendships across the usual barriers of age or culture.

Does this happen? Does it happen often enough? Or is our identity as a worldwide loving community being seriously and consistently undermined by the petty-minded squabbling, in-house bullying, pomposity and defensiveness which we allow ourselves to indulge in? Endemic grumbling and critical gossip are rife in the Church and they are deadly. Yet we still kid ourselves that these are not dangerous, 'heavyweight' sins, and we can live without tackling them too rigorously.

But it is for freedom that Christ has set us free. As the love community which willingly takes on the brokenness of Christ's loving, we are to see all our small-mindedness in the full light of God's nature, and hammer it to the cross for redeeming. It is nothing more or less than bread-breaking work, and to deny it is to deny our prayer for God's kingdom to come.

Discussion starters

1. How can service be freedom?
2. In the light of today's readings, what is your vision for the Church and where do we fall short of this?

Suggested order of service

Things to do and people to do them

The people and priest:

greet each other in the Lord's name
(this includes an introduction to this teaching Eucharist, and any practical details)

confess their sins and are assured of God's forgiveness
(an all-age introduction is suggested)

keep silence and pray a Collect

proclaim and respond to the Word of God

- 1 Kings 19:15-16, 19-21 – two voices are used in this reading
- Galatians 5:1, 13-25
- Luke 9:51-62 – the Gospel is read communally
- After the Gospel, Pebbles, Rocks, Boulders and adults respond to the Word in their own teaching, in separate parts of the church
- All-age talk draws these explorations together

pray for the Church and the world
(led by the Rocks with a visual focus for prayer)

exchange the Peace

prepare the table
(the Boulders help with this)

pray the Eucharistic Prayer
(the younger children are gathered around the altar)

receive Communion

depart with God's blessing
(everyone is signed with oil, anointing them for God's service as they leave the church)

Time of Confession and Forgiveness

Throughout the time of Confession the Pebbles group walk around the church with spirit levels, measuring the pews and floor to check they are 'true'.

(Voice 1)
If you live by the Spirit you must walk by the Spirit.

If you live by the Spirit you must walk by the Spirit.

(Voice 2)
Just as we can use a spirit level to measure our horizontals and check that the building is being properly built, so we need to apply the 'Spirit level' test to help us check our spiritual lives against the 'Spirit level' of our calling to be a freed community of love.

If you live by the Spirit you must walk by the Spirit.

(Voice 1)
Let us examine our thoughts, and the way we have become used to thinking, checking ourselves for right, good, loving thinking by the spirit level of the Spirit of God.

Silence

In sorrow for our sin we pray:
Lord, have mercy.

Lord, have mercy.

(Voice 2)
Let us examine our words and the way we have become used to speaking, checking ourselves for right, good, loving speaking by the spirit level of the Spirit of God.

Silence

In sorrow for our sin we pray:
Christ, have mercy.

Christ, have mercy.

(Voice 1)
Let us examine our deeds and the way we have become used to behaving, checking ourselves for right, good, loving action by the spirit level of the Spirit of God.

Silence

In sorrow for our sin we pray:
Lord, have mercy.

Lord, have mercy.

(The assurance of God's forgiveness is given.)

Old Testament reading

1 Kings 19:15-16, 19-21

Two people read the passage, while two more represent Elijah and Elisha. They can be dressed up appropriately. Elijah is wearing a cloak of some kind, and Elisha is not.

- Voice 1: verses 15-16. (Replace 'him' with 'Elijah' in verse 15.) Elijah is standing at the front on his own, facing the altar.
- Elijah walks down to the back of the church. Elisha emerges into the central aisle and stands there facing the front.
- Voice 1: verse 19. Elijah walks up from the back, throwing his cloak over Elisha as he passes him. Elijah continues to the front and stands with arms folded, waiting for Elisha.
- Voice 2: verse 20a (up to 'then I shall follow you'). Elisha runs up to the front and kneels facing Elijah with his arms out to him.
- Voice 1: verse 20b (starting 'Go back . . .'). Elijah opens arms as if to say, 'I'm not keeping you!'
- Voice 2: verse 21. Elisha runs down the aisle to the back of the church and out of sight. At the final sentence ('He then followed Elijah'), Elisha runs up the aisle to where Elijah is waiting and together they walk off, preferably a different way.

Gospel

Luke 9:51-62

This is a communal reading of the Gospel.

Ensure that everyone has a copy of the reading, clear enough for children as well as adults to read, and invite them all to walk with the Gospel reader either around the inside or the outside of the church, so that there is a sense of joining the crowd walking with Jesus.

You will need someone to read the words of Jesus, two adults to be James and John, and three others to be the other speakers mentioned. As you all set out, James and John are sent on ahead and come back with the news of rejection from the village. Everyone stops for this conversation (verses 54-55). The other people (from verse 57, 59 and 61) are sitting or standing at intervals along the route. The narrator leads the crowd to walk forward and stop for each of the conversations, with pauses where appropriate, before walking back to their own places.

Intercessions

The Rocks are leading the prayers today. The cloak used in the reading from 1 Kings is carried up to the front and laid over a chair in the aisle, as a focus.

The Rocks carry five banners made from A1 (flipchart size) paper, cut to cloak-shape, and cane as shown. As the prayers are read, the banners are carried from the main aisle to around the altar, where they are left for the rest of the service.

(Voice 1)
We have heard how Elijah threw his cloak over Elisha as a sign that he was being called to do an important job. Let us pray together now for all the work of God's people in the church and the world.

(When you hear us say: 'You are our God' will you respond: 'and we are your people'.)

You are our God:

and we are your people.

(Voice 2)
We pray for all who are called to follow Jesus,
that they may feel his cloak on their shoulders
and follow him faithfully each day of their lives.

Silence

You are our God:

and we are your people.

(Voice 3)
We pray for those who are called to be leaders in the world,
that they may be wise and good, fair and honest.

Silence

You are our God:

and we are your people.

(Voice 1)
We pray for those who are called to look after loved ones
and build up the local community,
that they may be filled with your love and kindness.

Silence

You are our God:

and we are your people.

(Voice 2)
We pray for those who are called to care
for those who are ill in body, mind or spirit,
that they may bring your healing love and comfort.

Silence

You are our God:

and we are your people.

(Voice 3)
We pray for those who have been called
into the fullness of life beyond death,
and for those who are sad because they miss them.
May they feel you there with them in their sadness.

Silence

You are our God:

and we are your people.

Merciful Father,

accept these prayers
for the sake of your Son,
our Saviour Jesus Christ. Amen.

The Anointing

Have several people take oil and a cloth and stand near the back of the church. As everyone leaves the church they are anointed with oil on the forehead in the shape of a cross, with the words: 'You belong to Christ. Go out in his name and share his love with all those you meet.'

All-age exploration of the Word
PEBBLES

Proper 8 – Year C

Sunday between 26 June and 2 July inclusive

Freed to serve

Thought for the day

Get rid of the old, imprisoning regime and let the new life of loving service liberate you to bear good fruit.

Readings

2 Kings 2:1-2, 6-14 or 1 Kings 19:15-16, 19-21
Psalm 77:1-2, 11-20 or Psalm 16
Galatians 5:1, 13-25
Luke 9:51-62

Before the service (advance preparation)

- Copy the sheets and prepare the area in church where the group will be working. You will need to fix a large brown trunk and green foliage to a pew or chair, and have ready some cut-out coloured fruits with glue to stick them on during the teaching. At the bottom of the tree trunk the paper extends as shown. It is folded up at the moment to look like part of the earth. During the teaching the earth flap is pulled down to reveal the roots. You also need a bowl of fresh fruit.

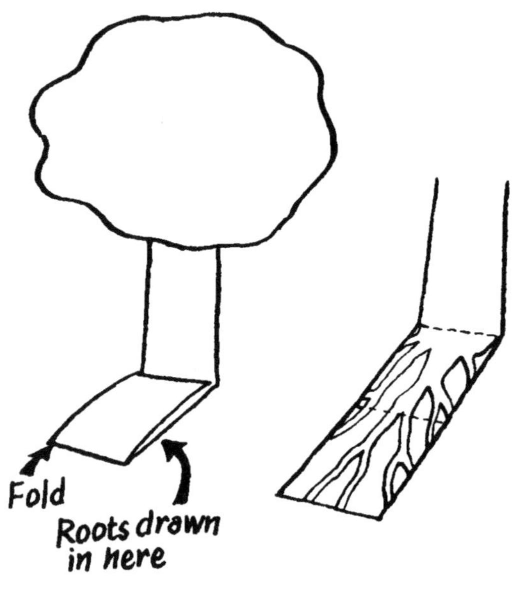

During the service

- The children help check the church furniture and floor with spirit levels during the time of repentance (they will each need a plastic water bottle almost full and a mark to show where the bubble should be on an exactly horizontal surface), and they take part in the communal reading of the Gospel walk.
- After the Gospel, gather the group in their work area in church.

Teaching
Show everyone the bowl of fruit, looking at each in turn and naming them. Where does fruit come from before it gets to the shops? It grows on good healthy trees.

Now show everyone our big tree, which hasn't got any fruit growing on it . . . yet!

Our lives can grow good fruit as well. It isn't fruit you can eat, it's spiritual fruit, and we're going to pretend this tree is like us, growing some good spiritual fruit. But it has to have strong roots if it's going to fruit. (Fold back the 'earth' to show that the tree is rooted in Jesus' love.) If we are going to be good fruiting trees we need to be rooted in Jesus' love as well.

Invite different children to stick on the cut-out fruits of love, joy, peace, patience, kindness, goodness, faithfulness, gentleness, and self-control. (As this is a very special tree the fruits can all be different colours and shapes if you like.)

Take another look at the tree's roots. The children can help stick on pictures of how we grow strong healthy roots – praying, coming to church and sharing the bread and wine or a blessing, reading about Jesus in the Bible, and practising saying 'No' to what is selfish and saying 'Yes' to what is loving.

On the sheet there is a big tree to colour in and the children can stick their own fruit on that. In Jesus we are set free to grow in love like tall trees, and our lives will grow lots of good fruit.

All together
The Pebbles will show their tree during the All-age Talk.

- At the Eucharistic prayer the children gather around the altar so that they can see what is going on and feel part of the community.

Notes

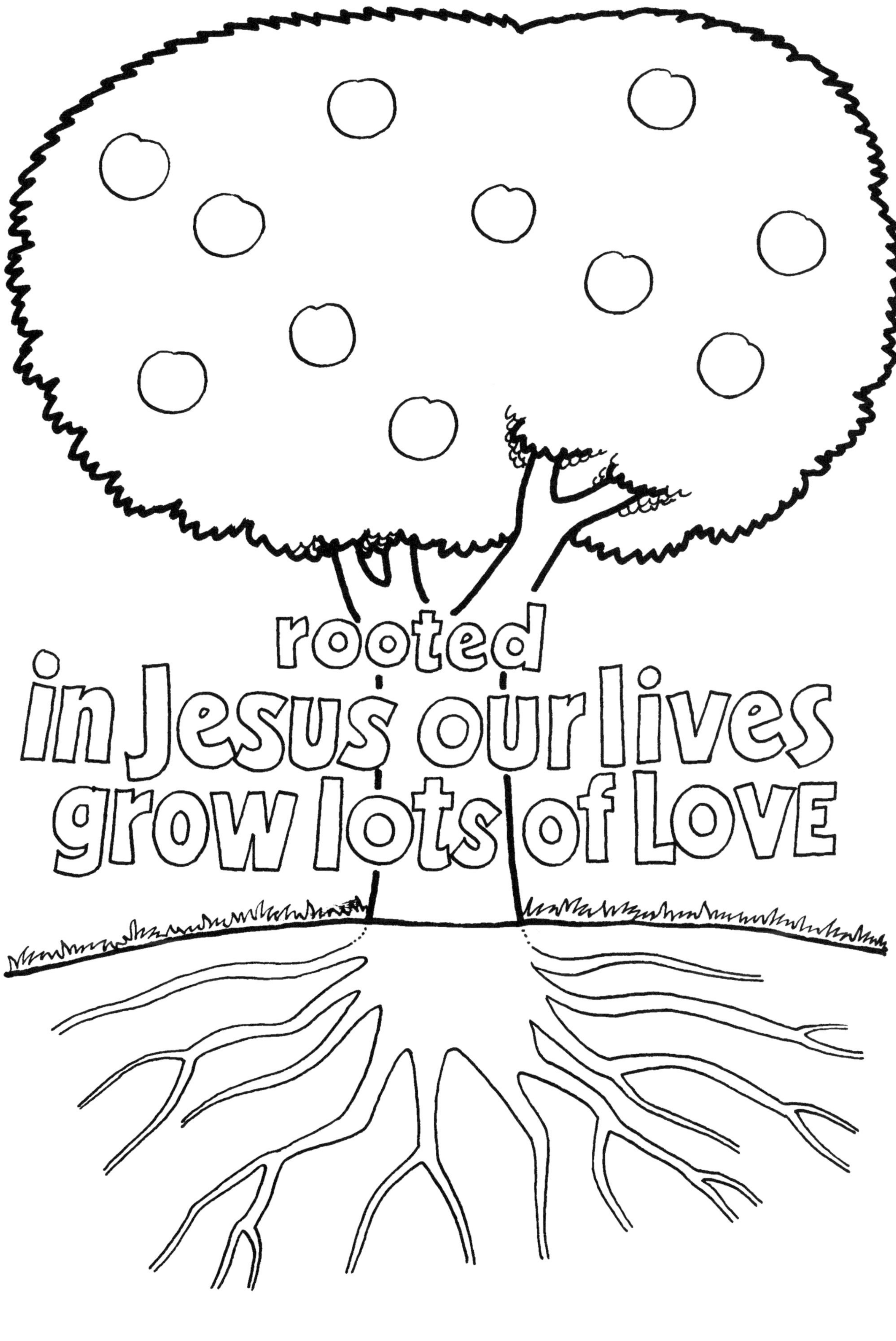
rooted
in Jesus our lives
grow lots of LOVE

All-age exploration of the Word
ROCKS

Proper 8 – Year C

Sunday between 26 June and 2 July inclusive

Freed to serve

Thought for the day

Get rid of the old, imprisoning regime and let the new life of loving service liberate you to bear good fruit.

Readings

2 Kings 2:1-2, 6-14 or 1 Kings 19:15-16, 19-21
Psalm 77:1-2, 11-20 or Psalm 16
Galatians 5:1, 13-25
Luke 9:51-62

Before the service (advance preparation)

- Copy the sheets and prepare the area where you will be working. You will also need five flipchart pages cut into cloak-shape as shown below, with the words of the prayers written in bubble writing on each, and a selection of chunky marker pens or crayons to colour them in and decorate them. Make copies of the suggested Intercessions on page 140 (enlarging the print to a suitable reading size) as the Rocks are leading the prayers today. The readers will need to practise so that they are confident and can use any sound system effectively.

- Two of the group may be representing Elijah and Elisha in the Old Testament reading; they will need to practise with the readers.

During the service

- The children will be taking part in the time of Confession and Forgiveness, and the communal Gospel walk.
- After the Gospel, gather the group in the working area.

Teaching
Remind the children of the Old Testament reading and help them work out the meaning of the 'throwing your cloak over someone' sign. (It was a sign of calling them and giving them power and authority for the job.)

As bread and wine people, we are called to work in the world to spread God's love wherever we go. On the sheet there are pictures going out from the Eucharist to show the church putting its love into action all over the world. These pictures can be used as a basis for discussion about how we can live out our Christian calling every day.

Share the colouring of the banners and practise the walking and reading, ready to lead the whole church in prayer.

All together
The Rocks will explain the symbols they have been using in their thinking about what the Church is called to be like.

- The Rocks are leading the Intercessions today.

Notes

Send us out in the power of your spirit
to live and work to your praise and glory.
Rose has come with Joel to visit Auntie in hospital.
Shourabh is working hard. He wants to be an engineer and help bring fresh water to the people in the villages of India.
Hospital ships sail to Africa and do operations to give people sight again.
Dan is teaching his brother to play football, while Mum helps Grandad with his gardening.
Irene is a lollipop lady outside the school. She likes making friends with the children and their mums and dads.
STOP
Dave drives a play-bus where children can come and learn about Jesus.
JESUS IS HERE

All-age exploration of the Word BOULDERS

Proper 8 – Year C

Sunday between 26 June and 2 July inclusive

Freed to serve

Thought for the day

Get rid of the old, imprisoning regime and let the new life of loving service liberate you to bear good fruit.

Readings

2 Kings 2:1-2, 6-14 or 1 Kings 19:15-16, 19-21
Psalm 77:1-2, 11-20 or Psalm 16
Galatians 5:1, 13-25
Luke 9:51-62

Before the service (advance preparation)

- Copy the sheets and prepare the area where you will be working. You will also need a large wooden cross made from discarded wood, some hammers and nails.
- If the group is involved in the acting of the Old Testament reading or the Gospel, they will need to practise this.

During the service

- The group will be taking part in the time of Confession and Forgiveness and the reading of the Gospel. Some may be reading in the Old Testament passage.
- After the Gospel, gather the group in the area where you are working.

Teaching
Talk over Elisha's calling and the weight of the cloak on his shoulders, as a sign of the responsibility of his calling. Our calling also carries a responsibility. Jesus doesn't call us to freedom in order to live as selfishly as possible, but in order to live as lovingly as we can.

Look over the reading from Galatians again, especially verse 13. This is written out on the sheet as well. We need to hammer our selfishness to the cross so that Jesus can deal with it for us and redeem it.

On the sheet there is the word 'Selfishness'. As they colour it in, cut it out and nail it to the cross, they think over the places in their own lives where selfishness rules, and bring this to Jesus for sorting it out.

All together
During the All-age Talk the Boulders' cross will be shown.

Notes

G	W	S	E	R	V	E	C	U	X	A	B
B	Y	Q	K	D	F	R	E	E	A	W	I
F	G	B	F	E	R	D	J	T	Z	F	M
W	K	R	V	R	E	M	Q	C	P	T	D
H	Z	O	P	A	E	E	W	L	T	E	V
B	L	T	S	L	D	H	C	G	L	U	K
R	E	H	X	N	O	E	T	L	U	K	T
J	Q	E	O	Z	M	I	A	O	F	V	B
C	X	R	A	R	N	C	P	H	N	U	O
S	H	S	T	D	J	Y	N	U	I	A	C
I	N	D	U	L	G	E	O	M	S	V	L
L	R	W	I	Q	S	M	X	B	G	E	D

CHRIST HAS SET US FREE

IF WE'RE SET FREE, DOES THAT MEAN WE'RE FREE TO DO WHATEVER WE LIKE?

Good question. To be free is often taken to mean behaving selfishly – and selfishness shuts us off from living the loving way.

YOU MEAN CHRIST HAS ACTUALLY SET US FREE FROM LIVING SELFISHLY?

Impossible as it may seem, yes, he has. In Christ we are set free to love people like God does.

IT'LL TAKE QUITE A LOT TO STOP ME BEING SELF-CENTRED, I'M AFRAID.

That goes for all of us. But with God some things are not just possible but natural.

YOU, MY BR______, WERE C____D TO BE F___. BUT DO NOT U__ YOUR FR____M TO IN___G_ THE S____L NATURE; RATHER, S__V_ ONE AN_____ IN L___

AS YOU COLOUR THIS IN AND HAMMER IT TO THE CROSS, FACE UP TO THE PLACES IN YOUR OWN LIFE WHERE **SELF** IS FIRMLY AT THE CENTRE.

All-age exploration of the Word
ADULTS

Proper 8 – Year C

Sunday between 26 June and 2 July inclusive

Freed to serve

Notes

Thought for the day

Get rid of the old, imprisoning regime and let the new life of loving service liberate you to bear good fruit.

Readings

2 Kings 2:1-2, 6-14 or 1 Kings 19:15-16, 19-21
Psalm 77:1-2, 11-20 or Psalm 16
Galatians 5:1, 13-25
Luke 9:51-62

Before the service (advance preparation)

- Copy the sheets and prepare a sheet of flipchart paper labelled 'Symbols of our vision for the Church'. You will also need coloured pens for each person in the group.
- Two people need to prepare the time of Penitence.
- Some adults will be involved in acting out the readings and will need to practise this.

During the service

- They will be taking part in the time of Confession and Forgiveness, and the communal Gospel walk.
- After the Gospel, the adults break into small groups with an enabler to explore the readings.

Teaching
Recall today's readings, sharing any particular verses which they have found helpful or challenging. Read the reflection on the readings and use the discussion starters. In the light of your discussion, think of some symbols for the vision of the Church and draw them on the sheet.

All together
During the All-age Talk the adults will show their drawings and share their thinking about the Church.

Freed to serve

Thought for the day

Get rid of the old, imprisoning regime and let the new life of loving service liberate you to bear good fruit.

Reflection on the readings

2 Kings 2:1-2, 6-14 or
1 Kings 19:15-16, 19-21
Psalm 77:1-2, 11-20 or Psalm 16
Galatians 5:1, 13-25
Luke 9:51-62

What does it mean for us to be 'bread and wine people'? Are we a religious club? Illusioned comfort-cravers? Morality activists? Reality refusers? Historical costume freaks? Or what? Perhaps we must shamefacedly admit that we are indeed all these here and there and from time to time, just as we are so often perceived and portrayed. But we know equally well that these models are nothing like our calling, or what the Church at its most authentic can be.

Today's readings give us some idea of what we are really called to be, and we need courage to read them candidly because they make uncomfortable and challenging reading. If, as followers of Christ, we have indeed allowed our sin-directed nature to be crucified, shouldn't the results show?

We should expect to find in this community of Christ-followers young, tender shoots and healthy maturing trees, vigorous fruiting and strong root systems. We might expect to find ourselves violently disliked and disapproved of by the worldly for our refusal as a community to comply with corruption and injustice, and for ruffling feathers wherever oppression rules and validity is sidelined.

At the same time we might expect to find a regular flow of enquirers drawn to this vibrant, alternative community, fascinated by the way we are able to live in love, even where there is strong disagreement, and by the unusually simple, uncomplicated way we warmly respond to needs without complex sub-agendas, and by the infectious, good-natured fun and open friendships across the usual barriers of age or culture.

Does this happen? Does it happen often enough? Or is our identity as a worldwide loving community being seriously and consistently undermined by the petty-minded squabbling, in-house bullying, pomposity and defensiveness which we allow ourselves to indulge in? Endemic grumbling and critical gossip are rife in the Church and they are deadly. Yet we still kid ourselves that these are not dangerous, 'heavyweight' sins, and we can live without tackling them too rigorously.

But it is for freedom that Christ has set us free. As the love community which willingly takes on the brokenness of Christ's loving, we are to see all our small-mindedness in the full light of God's nature, and hammer it to the cross for redeeming. It is nothing more or less than bread-breaking work, and to deny it is to deny our prayer for God's kingdom to come.

Discussion starters

1. How can service be freedom?
2. In the light of today's readings, what is your vision for the Church and where do we fall short of this?

All-age talk

(Everyone in the church has been exploring the Word of God and this talk enables them to learn from one another.)

Bring along several balls of coloured wool or string.

Ask a few people (different age groups, including adults) to represent our church community by standing together at the altar. Give someone else the balls of wool or string, and ask them to stay at the altar holding the ends tightly, while the people in our church move away, unravelling the wool/ string as they go. This is what happens every week – we gather around the altar and share the bread and wine, and then go off in our different directions into our various jobs and relationships during the rest of the week.

But the love of God stays with us, binding us together with God and one another even when we are outside the church building, busy at school or work, talking with our friends, making choices, avoiding temptation, and generally bringing God's love out into the whole world. The love of God which binds us is strong and flexible, and never gets tangled up or broken, and when we come back the next week we bring with us to the altar (the representatives gather up their lengths of wool/string as they gather again) all that has gone on during the week. Some of it we bring for healing, some to say thank you, some to say sorry, and God deals with it all. It's like a great tide of love that flows in and out over the people we meet, and our work as Christians is to bring in the aches and hurts and joys of those we meet and bring out the healing love to them week by week by week.

How does it work? The Pebbles can show us. (They bring their tree.) Each one of us is like a tree bearing lots of love-fruits which spread God's love by the way we live. Things like love, joy, peace, patience, kindness, goodness, faithfulness, gentleness and self-control. And the secret of good fruit is to have really good roots. (Open the flap to see what the Pebbles have drawn – prayer, worship together, reading the Bible and practising our loving.)

What about the darker side of us, though? All that selfishness which we know often messes up our good intentions and makes us cut ourselves off from God's love? The older ones among us know that selfishness isn't something we eventually just grow out of – we *all* have to go on battling with it all our lives.

Invite the Boulders to bring their cross. What was it they were hammering to the cross earlier on? It's selfishness, and that's what we all need to keep doing – hammering our selfishness to the cross so that Jesus can deal with it and set us free again to spread God's love.

The adults and the Rocks have been thinking of signs and symbols for what the church is called to be like. The Rocks will be leading us in our prayers to think of our calling as a cloak placed on our shoulders, setting us apart for this special work of loving. And the adults have been coming up with some other ideas as well. (Invite the group leaders to show some of the drawings.)

So as we gather around the table and share the bread and wine today, and then leave the church to go out in the power of God's love, let's remember that we are still joined on to God's love, and we are called as a church not to argue and grumble and want our own way all the time, but to spread the healing love of God to everyone we meet throughout the coming week.

Proper 25 – Year C

Sunday between 23 and 29 October inclusive

Depending on God for everything

Thought for the day

We owe our entire existence to God's faithful, generous love. In each Eucharist we celebrate Jesus saving us by doing for us on the cross what we can never do for ourselves.

Reflection on the readings

Joel 2:23-32 or Jeremiah 14:7-10, 19-22
Psalm 65 or Psalm 84:1-7
2 Timothy 4:6-8, 16-18
Luke 18:9-14

However much we may decide not to believe in God, God never stops believing in us. That is partly because, like God, we really exist, and since God is truth, his nature is to acknowledge what is true. But God believing in us is also a mark of his extraordinary love, because in spite of all the pain and anguish we cause our Creator by the destructive choices we make and the opportunities we reject, God never ever gives up on us and decides we are a bad idea. He proved that when he broke into our humanness to rescue us through the person of Jesus. The echoes of that cosmic cry of love are still reverberating and will do so for ever, and we tune into it with particular focus at every Eucharist.

The truth is that we and the universe we inhabit only exist through God's choice, so that, like it or not, we are only independent within the framework of our basic dependence on God. The irony is that the more we recognise our dependence on God, the more free and independent as people we are able to become; it is knowing our need of God which actually enables us to become more fully ourselves. And it is in the knowledge of God's love for us that we summon the courage to admit to our need of God.

As a Eucharistic community we recognise that we are a body of students, learning to stand on our own feet, while conscious that those feet have been created by the God we worship, so it is only in his love and power that we stand at all. As we sometimes say at the offertory, 'All good things come from you and of your own do we give you.'

Such knowledge helps our humility. Whenever we remember our basic dependence on God's love, we are reminded of who we are – not gods, but lovingly created human beings. It lifts the pressure of striving for what we can never become, and lets us value and enjoy what we are. Humility allows us to put an end to the effort of pretence and keeping up appearances because in humility we can simply be ourselves – candid and straightforward, admitting to mistakes and open to others, with no further need to be defensive.

Regular feeding with the bread of life deepens the consciousness of our dependence on God for everything in life – physical and spiritual. Each Eucharist, as we call to mind the last supper and Jesus' giving of his life for us in love, we celebrate our dependence on God. As we grow in that knowledge we will grow in the 'travel light' grace of humility and discover a new and radical kind of freedom in the process.

Discussion starters

1. Would an alien visiting the planet notice anything about the way Christians live which might point to them realising their dependence on God?
2. Which situations remind us of our need of God and which give us a false sense of superiority and independence of him?
3. How does Holy Communion reinforce our interdependence on God and one another?

Suggested order of service

Things to do and people to do them

The people and priest:

greet each other in the Lord's name
(this includes an introduction to this teaching Eucharist and any practical details)

confess their sins and are assured of God's forgiveness
(the Boulders lead this today)

keep silence and pray a Collect

proclaim and respond to the Word of God
- Joel 2:23-32 – this passage is read communally
- 2 Timothy 4:6-8, 16-18
- Luke 18:9-14 – the Gospel is read by a narrator and three other people
- After the Gospel, Pebbles, Rocks, Boulders and adults explore the Word in their own teaching, in different parts of the church
- All-age Talk draws these explorations together

pray for the Church and the world
(led by representatives from the different groups, and accompanied with projected images)

exchange the Peace

prepare the table
(the Rocks help with this today)

pray the Eucharistic Prayer
(the younger children are gathered around the altar)

receive Communion

depart with God's blessing

Time of Confession and Forgiveness

The Boulders lead this today. As everyone comes into church they are given a paper cut-out anchor. If possible, the Boulders have a real anchor at the front of the church – otherwise a life-size cardboard version on a length of paper chain.

(Voice 1)
Lives that are anchored firm and deep
in the love of God
need never be shaken by the storms and raging sea.

(Voice 2)
For the times we have put our trust in other things
and other people instead of God,
we are sorry and ask your forgiveness.

Lord, have mercy.
Lord, have mercy.

(Voice 3)
For the times we have deliberately turned
away from God
in thought, word or action,
we are sorry and ask your forgiveness.

Christ, have mercy.
Christ, have mercy.

(Voice 4)
For the times we have chosen
what we know to be wrong,
we are sorry and ask your forgiveness.

Lord, have mercy.
Lord, have mercy.

(Voice 1)
Lives that are anchored firm and deep
in the love of God
need never again be shaken
by the storms and raging sea.

(The people are assured of God's forgiveness.)

Old Testament reading

Joel 2:23-32

Ensure that everyone has a copy of this reading which is on page 155.

Gospel

Luke 18:9-14

- Luke, holding a clipboard and pen, reads verse 9.
- Jesus walks to the front and tells or reads the story, indicating the Pharisee and the tax-collector as they come in, one either side of him. Each of them prays his own prayer while Jesus watches and listens to them.
- At verse 14a Jesus moves over to the tax-collector until both prayers go home, leaving Jesus to give the story's teaching in verse 14b.

Intercessions

(A young person)
Everything that exists comes from God.
Let us pray to him now.

(A man)
Help us, Lord, to be aware of your love,
all the time and everywhere,
so that we live in you and you in us.

(A woman)
Day by day may we love you more and more,
and learn to trust in you.

(A child)
May the way we live help other people
to get to know you better.

Silence

(A young person)
We pray for the world we live in
and all who share it with us;
we pray for the leaders of the nations
and all who have power and authority.

(A man)
Help us to share the world's resources fairly
so that we all have enough
and no one is left hungry or thirsty.

Silence

(A woman)
We pray for our families and our friends,
that we may treat one another with love and respect.

(A child)
Help us to forgive one another
and look after one another.

Silence

(A young person)
We pray for those who are ill and in pain,
and for those who are sad or frightened.

(A man)
Surround them with your love and comfort,
and bring them healing.

Silence

(A woman)
We pray for those who have died,
that they may be with you for ever.

(A child)
Protect us all from evil
and lead us to walk in your love
all the days of our life.

Silence

Merciful Father,
accept these prayers
for the sake of your Son,
our Saviour Jesus Christ. Amen.

Communal reading of Joel 2:23-32

All **O children of Zion, be glad and rejoice in the Lord your God;**

Men for he has given the early rain for your vindication,

Women he has poured down for you abundant rain,

Children the early and the later rain, as before.

All **The threshing floors shall be full of grain,**
the vats shall overflow with wine and oil.

Men I will repay you for the years that the swarming locust has eaten,

Children the hopper, the destroyer, and the cutter,

Men my great army, which I sent against you.

Women You shall eat in plenty and be satisfied,
and praise the name of the Lord your God,
who has dealt wondrously with you.

Men And my people shall never again be put to shame.

All **You shall know that I am in the midst of Israel,**
and that I, the Lord, am your God and there is no other.

Men And my people shall never again be put to shame.

Children Then afterwards I will pour out my spirit on all flesh;

Women your sons and your daughters shall prophesy,

Men your old men shall dream dreams,
and your young men shall see visions.

Women Even on the male and female slaves,
in those days, I will pour out my spirit.

Men I will show portents in the heavens and on the earth,
blood, fire and columns of smoke.

All **The sun shall be turned to darkness, and the moon to blood,**
before the great and terrible day of the Lord comes.

Children Then everyone who calls on the name of the Lord shall be saved;

All **for in Mount Zion and in Jerusalem**
there shall be those who escape, as the Lord has said,
and among the survivors shall be those whom the Lord calls.

All-age exploration of the Word
PEBBLES

Proper 25 – Year C

Sunday between 23 and 29 October inclusive

Depending on God for everything

Thought for the day

We owe our entire existence to God's faithful, generous love. In each Eucharist we celebrate Jesus saving us by doing for us on the cross what we can never do for ourselves.

Readings

Joel 2:23-32 or Jeremiah 14:7-10, 19-22
Psalm 65 or Psalm 84:1-7
2 Timothy 4:6-8, 16-18
Luke 18:9-14

Before the service (advance preparation)

- Copy the sheets and prepare the area in which you will be working. Bring along an assortment of objects such as a tin of baked beans, a plastic toy, an item of cotton clothing, something made of wood and something of metal. You will also need some photographs of people.

During the service

- After the Gospel gather the children in their work area.

Teaching
Spread out the objects on the floor and talk about where they have come from. Everything comes from something on our planet Earth – God has given us all the things we need, because he loves us. And we can use everything he gives us to make lots of other things as well! On their sheet there are dot-to-dot pictures to complete of things made from trees, rock and animals – all part of God's creation.

We are made by God as well (show the photographs) so we depend on God for everything. People can't make something from nothing – only God can make from nothing. Only God can give life which goes on even after our bodies die. (Place down a cross.) Only God can turn us into loving people.

When we share the bread and wine together at Communion, we are sharing Jesus' life, and that is the life which goes on even after our bodies die.

All together
During the All-age Talk the children will be shown the objects and asked where they all come from, so that everyone can share the truth of our dependence on God for everything.

Notes

Everything comes from
GOD

All-age exploration of the Word ROCKS

Proper 25 – Year C

Sunday between 23 and 29 October inclusive

Depending on God for everything

Thought for the day

We owe our entire existence to God's faithful, generous love. In each Eucharist we celebrate Jesus saving us by doing for us on the cross what we can never do for ourselves.

Readings

Joel 2:23-32 or Jeremiah 14:7-10, 19-22
Psalm 65 or Psalm 84:1-7
2 Timothy 4:6-8, 16-18
Luke 18:9-14

Before the service (advance preparation)

- Copy the sheets and prepare the area in which you will be working. You will need a picture of baby birds being fed, and two simple puppets to represent the Pharisee and the tax-collector. These can be made from a wooden spoon or spatula.
- Make copies of the communal Old Testament reading.
- One or two of the children will be helping to lead the Intercessions and will need to practise this.

During the service

- The children will be taking part in the communal reading of the Old Testament reading.
- After the Gospel, gather the group in their working area.

Teaching
Using simple puppets and Bibles to refer to, talk over the gospel and the story Jesus told in it. Help them recall the different ways in which the Pharisee and the tax-collector prayed, and what Jesus had to say about that. Why was it that the sins of the tax-collector were forgiven, rather than those of the Pharisee?

What about us as we come to Communion? How might we come like the Pharisee? How might we come like the tax-collector? (Make up some appropriate 'Pharisee prayers' together. There is space on the sheets for this.)

Show a picture of baby birds with their beaks open, being fed by the parent bird. When we come to Communion we come knowing that we depend on God for everything. We know our need of God, so we come asking for his forgiveness, and for the grace to be healed and loving people, made strong ready for the week ahead, so that we can go out and serve others in the power of God's love.

All together
In the all-age talk the Rocks show their picture of the baby birds, and they can also read out their Pharisee prayers.

- One or two Rocks are helping to lead the Intercessions

Notes

LORD HAVE MERCY

How NOT to pray!

O Lord, I thank you that I'm better than most people.

I ________________

____

____

____

____

Jesus said

When you pray, don't tell God how good you are. Remember that you need his mercy and forgiveness . . .

God loves us and provides all our needs

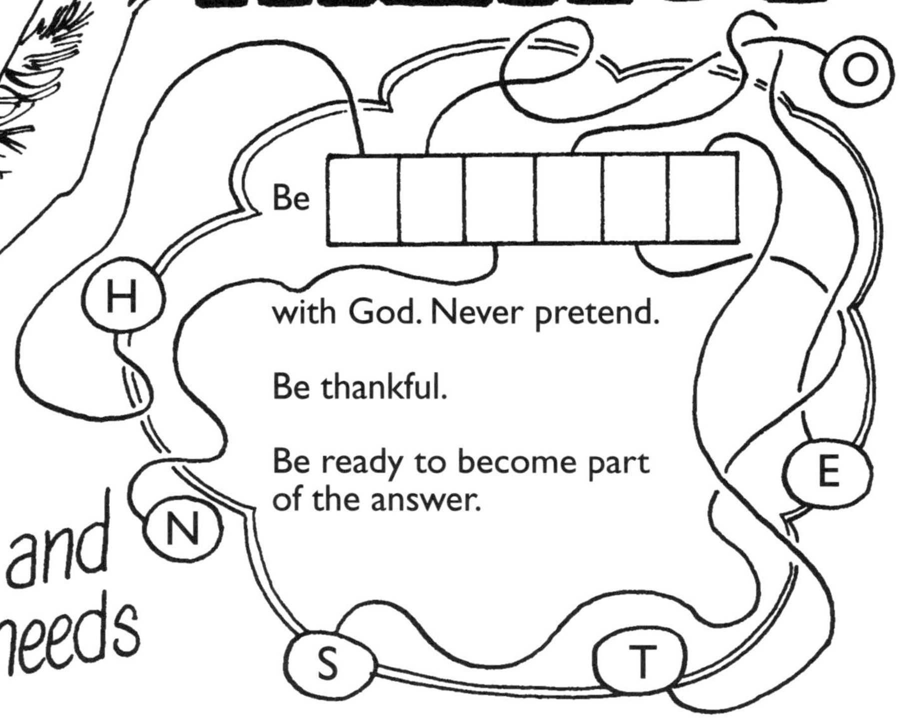

All-age exploration of the Word
BOULDERS

Proper 25 – Year C

Sunday between 23 and 29 October inclusive

Depending on God for everything

Thought for the day

We owe our entire existence to God's faithful, generous love. In each Eucharist we celebrate Jesus saving us by doing for us on the cross what we can never do for ourselves.

Readings

Joel 2:23-32 or Jeremiah 14:7-10, 19-22
Psalm 65 or Psalm 84:1-7
2 Timothy 4:6-8, 16-18
Luke 18:9-14

Before the service (advance preparation)

- Copy the sheets and prepare the area in which you will be working.
- The group are leading the time of penitence, and will need to prepare a cut-out anchor for everyone in church and, if possible, borrow a real anchor as well.
- They will be taking part in the communal Old Testament reading and will need copies of this (see page 155).
- Some of the Boulders may be taking part in the Gospel reading, and the Intercessions.

During the service

- Some of the group are leading the Time of Penitence.
- They will all be taking part in the communal reading of the Old Testament passage.
- One or two may be involved in the Gospel reading and the Intercessions.
- After the Gospel, gather the group in their work area.

Teaching

Talk over the Gospel and the parable told by Jesus. What does Luke say was the reason for Jesus telling this story? Why does he choose a Pharisee and a tax-collector as his characters? (The Pharisee represented the good and upright church leaders, respected for their supposed holiness. The tax-collector represented the opposite – the last people Jesus' listeners would have expected to be heard by God and forgiven.)

On the sheet are some quotations from church people and others outside the church. Look at these and think about how we can all easily slip into hypocrite or self-exalt modes if we aren't careful. What stops us doing this is recognising our real need of God.

(Place down an empty box.) When we come to Communion, we know we come empty and ready to receive God's love. As soon as we start thinking ourselves above that, we start blocking our reception channels (close the box up), and then God's love can't get in to help us, any more than it could help the Pharisee while he was simply glorying in his own splendid achievements.

As a Eucharistic community, our dependence on God should show in the choices we make, the way we react to difficulties, and the way we organise our finances. Work out what these might be; how does trusting God affect our lifestyle?

All together

During the All-age Talk the empty box will be used, and the group asked to explain how we need to come to God empty, ready to receive God's love.

Notes

KNOW THAT I AM GOD

IF GOD HADN'T BROUGHT THIS UNIVERSE INTO BEING, IT WOULDN'T BE HERE, RIGHT?

Right! We owe our total existence and cosmic environment to God's love.

HOW COME SO MANY PEOPLE IGNORE THE GOD WHO KEEPS THEM AND MADE THEM?

Lots of people have never yet come across the real living God. They think we invented God, rather than the other way round.

HOW DOES GOD FEEL ABOUT THAT? DOESN'T IT MAKE HIM REALLY SAD?

Well, we can see how much he loves us when we look at Jesus. There on the cross is love and sorrow mixed together.

All-age exploration of the Word
ADULTS

Proper 25 – Year C

Sunday between 23 and 29 October inclusive

Depending on God for everything

Thought for the day

We owe our entire existence to God's faithful, generous love. In each Eucharist we celebrate Jesus saving us by doing for us on the cross what we can never do for ourselves.

Readings

Joel 2:23-32 or Jeremiah 14:7-10, 19-22
Psalm 65 or Psalm 84:1-7
2 Timothy 4:6-8, 16-18
Luke 18:9-14

Before the service (advance preparation)

- Copy the sheets for your group. All the group enablers will need pens, a flipchart-sized sheet of paper headed: 'A community dependent on God?', and an empty chalice and patten.
- Prepare copies of the communal Old Testament reading.
- Organise who is going to take part in the Gospel reading and practise it.
- Some adults will be helping to lead the Intercessions.

During the service

- Some adults will be taking part in the Old Testament reading, the Gospel reading and the Intercessions.
- After the Gospel, the adults split into small groups all over the church.

Teaching
Begin by referring to today's readings, and sharing any words or phrases which people find especially speaking to them. Look together at the reflection on the readings and then use the discussion starters, keeping track of points made on the large sheet of paper, either in words or symbols.

Use the empty chalice to help people focus on the way we come to God empty and he fills us with his forgiving, healing love. He feeds us with his life which lasts for ever.

All together
During the All-age Talk the group will share the symbol of the empty chalice.

Notes

Depending on God for everything

Thought for the day

We owe our entire existence to God's faithful, generous love. In each Eucharist we celebrate Jesus saving us by doing for us on the cross what we can never do for ourselves.

Reflection on the readings

Joel 2:23-32 or Jeremiah 14:7-10, 19-22
Psalm 65 or Psalm 84:1-7
2 Timothy 4:6-8, 16-18
Luke 18:9-14

However much we may decide not to believe in God, God never stops believing in us. That is partly because, like God, we really exist, and since God is truth, his nature is to acknowledge what is true. But God believing in us is also a mark of his extraordinary love, because in spite of all the pain and anguish we cause our Creator by the destructive choices we make and the opportunities we reject, God never ever gives up on us and decides we are a bad idea. He proved that when he broke into our humanness to rescue us through the person of Jesus. The echoes of that cosmic cry of love are still reverberating and will do so for ever, and we tune into it with particular focus at every Eucharist.

The truth is that we and the universe we inhabit only exist through God's choice, so that, like it or not, we are only independent within the framework of our basic dependence on God. The irony is that the more we recognise our dependence on God, the more free and independent as people we are able to become; it is knowing our need of God which actually enables us to become more fully ourselves. And it is in the knowledge of God's love for us that we summon the courage to admit to our need of God.

As a Eucharistic community we recognise that we are a body of students, learning to stand on our own feet, while conscious that those feet have been created by the God we worship, so it is only in his love and power that we stand at all. As we sometimes say at the offertory, 'All good things come from you and of your own do we give you.'

Such knowledge helps our humility. Whenever we remember our basic dependence on God's love, we are reminded of who we are – not gods, but lovingly created human beings. It lifts the pressure of striving for what we can never become, and lets us value and enjoy what we are. Humility allows us to put an end to the effort of pretence and keeping up appearances because in humility we can simply be ourselves – candid and straightforward, admitting to mistakes and open to others, with no further need to be defensive.

Regular feeding with the bread of life deepens the consciousness of our dependence on God for everything in life – physical and spiritual. Each Eucharist, as we call to mind the last supper and Jesus' giving of his life for us in love, we celebrate our dependence on God. As we grow in that knowledge we will grow in the 'travel light' grace of humility and discover a new and radical kind of freedom in the process.

Discussion starters

1. Would an alien visiting the planet notice anything about the way Christians live which might point to them realising their dependence on God?
2. Which situations remind us of our need of God and which give us a false sense of superiority and independence of him?
3. How does Holy Communion reinforce our interdependence on God and one another?

All-age talk

(Everyone in church has been exploring the Word of God and this talk enables them to learn from one another.)

Begin by showing everyone the anchor and explaining how it works by jamming into the rocks or mud and holding a boat firm, so that it doesn't drift away. As Christians, we know our lives and our universe are anchored firmly in God's love, so that we are held safe in this life we are given.

Invite the Pebbles to show some of their objects, and ask them where they have come from. (It always leads back to God.) We know that as part of creation, we all depend on God for everything.

Or do we know it? Do we sometimes think and talk and live as if we are the gods and know everything; as if it's all our cleverness and skill which keeps the world going, and we can live as we please because God is only there if we bother to believe in him. There is a real danger that even when we are baptised Christians, and have committed ourselves to Christ, we can get into that worldly way of thinking and just change the language into churchy things.

Invite the Rocks to share some of the 'Pharisee prayers' they have made up.

Today's readings make us look at whether we are slipping into that rather smug, showing-off mode. If we are, it isn't the end of the world. It just means that we need to go back to God and tell him we are sorry and want to put things right again. (Invite the Boulders to bring their empty box and the adults an empty chalice.) As soon as we come to God not pretending we're full, but knowing we're empty, God can start filling us with his love.

As we come to receive Communion today, and week by week, let's come knowing that we need God's love and forgiveness, thanking him for saving us, and asking him into our lives.

Section Two
THE ANNUAL MEALS

The Fellowship Meal

Introduction and preparation

The date of this meal is entirely up to you and your parish. You might consider making it the Dedication, Patronal Festival or Harvest meal, or part of a parish weekend. This is *not* a Eucharist, and should be a time when non-churchgoing family members are encouraged to come. The atmosphere is informal and friendly, and the food suitable for all ages. The teaching takes place between courses, and should be entertaining as well as informative and thought-provoking. Everyone takes some part in the preparation of the evening.

There are short sketches to be rehearsed beforehand, games to be organised and song words to be duplicated or projected. Keyboard, simple recorder and violin, and guitar parts are provided so that all ages can take part in the music making. Children's, young people's and adults' recipes are given, as are instructions for place settings and room decoration. Adult, young person, child and toddler place mats are all photocopiable.

The evening's menu – example

Menu

The Grace

The first course
Dips and Dippers

A musical interlude

The main course
Pizza companiere – Mixed salad
Jacket potato – Home-made bread rolls

A dramatic interlude

Our just desserts
All sweet and delicious

So this is our church

After-dinner drinks and sweets

The welcome

A mixed age-group of those who usually welcome people into church and give out hymn books are there at the hall door, welcoming each person by name with a handshake. (This includes greeting each of the children by name.) Each person is given a short length of coloured wool and a flower or sprig of greenery.

Trays of drinks are handed round. During this time, everyone finds at least two other people with the same colour wool, and exchanges names and favourite colours.

Setting the table

Think about the way tables are set out in the room; aim to reflect a sense of community and equality. Here are some possibilities to consider.

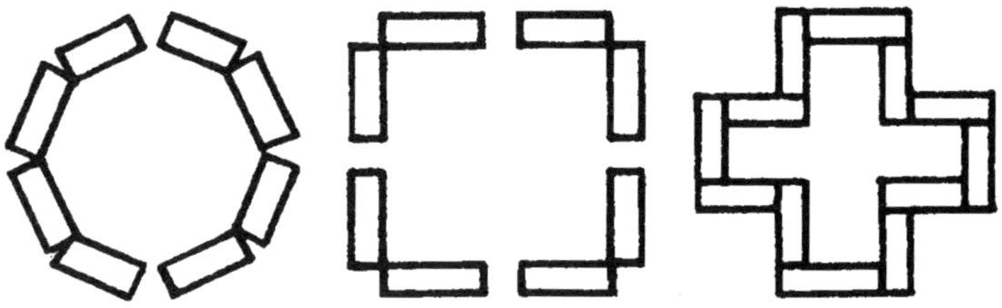

Tables are laid out with place names and age-appropriate place mats (see pages 176-179). (Ask everyone a week or so ahead if they have any special preferences for table companions, and try to ensure a mixing of ages, so that no one is isolated.)

There are small vases filled with water and pots of coloured and lead pencils for use with the place-mat activities. Young people and children direct and help people to their places. On each section of table there is a 'menu' which includes

activities as well as food and drink. By the vase is an invitation to make a table decoration using the sprigs of greenery and flowers which each person was given when they arrived. As each person adds a sprig to the collective arrangement, they share something they love doing and something they hate having to do.

The Grace

Blessed are you, Lord God of all creation.
Of your goodness we have this food to enjoy,
which earth has given and human hands have made.
Blessed be God for ever. Amen.

The first course

A selection of dips with dishes of assorted crisps, carrot and celery sticks, cauliflower florets, sliced peppers and cucumber, and mushrooms. Clues to the puzzles on the place mats are given on the doily under the vegetables (see page 171) so that they emerge during the eating.

A musical interlude

A communal piece of music led by a mixed age group of musicians. This can be any fairly simple melody, preferably a round, which opens up all kinds of communal possibilities, and to which percussion instruments can be added. I have included the music for a round – 'Rejoice in the Lord always' – and one traditional melody – 'The Ash Grove'. Simple parts are provided for recorder and violin. (See pages 196-200.)

The main course

Whatever you choose as your main course, give it an appropriate name, and write out the recipe to include prayer as an integral part of the preparation. I have given two prayer-worked recipes in full to give you the idea. (See pages 172 and 173). Give out the recipe and ingredients to the chefs – one chef for every eight people. They either make the food at the hall or prepare the main course and bring it to the hall for heating through. In the same way, have one salad maker for each eight diners. The bread rolls are made by the children.

A dramatic interlude

A group of young people perform a short sketch on the theme of community and recognising one another's validity. Use the sketch on pages 174 and 175.

Our just desserts

An assortment of desserts to which people help themselves. People other than the main course chefs will have made the desserts, so that the workload is evenly spread.

So this is our church

This is a visual presentation of the past year of the church community, and the aim is to show that our worship in church gathers together and focuses all the variety of everyone's lives, empowering us to live in the real world as Christians. The more people shown in the pictures, the better.

There need to be visual memories of all the different events throughout the year, interspersed with pictures of different groups of people of all ages who are part of the community, doing their ordinary things, like walking to school, travelling to work, working, playing, shopping, and relaxing. In between all of this are pictures of people in all seasons going in to church and coming out, worshipping together in church and in small groups, reading the Bible and praying.

Sharing in such an experience will help develop the sense of community, as everyone loves seeing themselves and their friends and family. Without using any words at all the pictures communicate the love and affection of your church community, and open people's eyes to the way we are Christians living out our faith seven days a week rather than just in church on a Sunday.

To prepare for this:

- Appoint a camera team to take pictures throughout the year, both of the church and events, and of people living their lives.
- Decide on which method of presentation will be best for you, depending on the technical wizardry of those in the parish. Bear in mind that young people are particularly good at working on effective presentations like this, and have a great deal of expertise.
- You could use slides projected on to a screen, photographs scanned on to acetates and projected using an OHP, or a cumulative video shown either on a television or using a video projector. A PowerPoint presentation using a collection of scanned photographs can also be projected in this way. Alternatively, create a display around the room with pictures mounted imaginatively. Enlargements can be made quite cheaply by scanning or colour photocopying.

After dinner drinks and sweets

While women and girls distribute drinks, dishes of sweets made by the men and boys are distributed to each section of the table. Each sweet is in a small paper case on which is written a Bible reference. Bibles are available so that everyone can look up their verses.

Here are the Bible references:

Matthew 5:11-12
Matthew 5:14-16
Matthew 5:43-45
Matthew 6:24
Matthew 6:31-33
Matthew 7:7-8
Matthew 11:28-30
Matthew 12:48-50
Mark 9:35
Mark 9:36-37
Mark 10:15
Mark 10:51
Mark 11:25
Mark 12:17
Mark 14:38
Luke 6:36
Luke 9:23-24
Luke 9:35
Luke 10:2
Luke 12:32-34
Luke 18:15-16
Luke 19:8-10
Luke 22:19
Luke 23:34
Luke 24:46-47
John 1:14
John 3:16

Go in peace

To conclude the celebration, there is a script which everyone takes part in. Words are printed on the place mats, so that each person knows when to join in with their part. As everyone leaves, the welcoming party are there to say goodbye personally and give each one a small gift, together with an invitation to the next training Eucharist.

Doily for the first-course vegetables

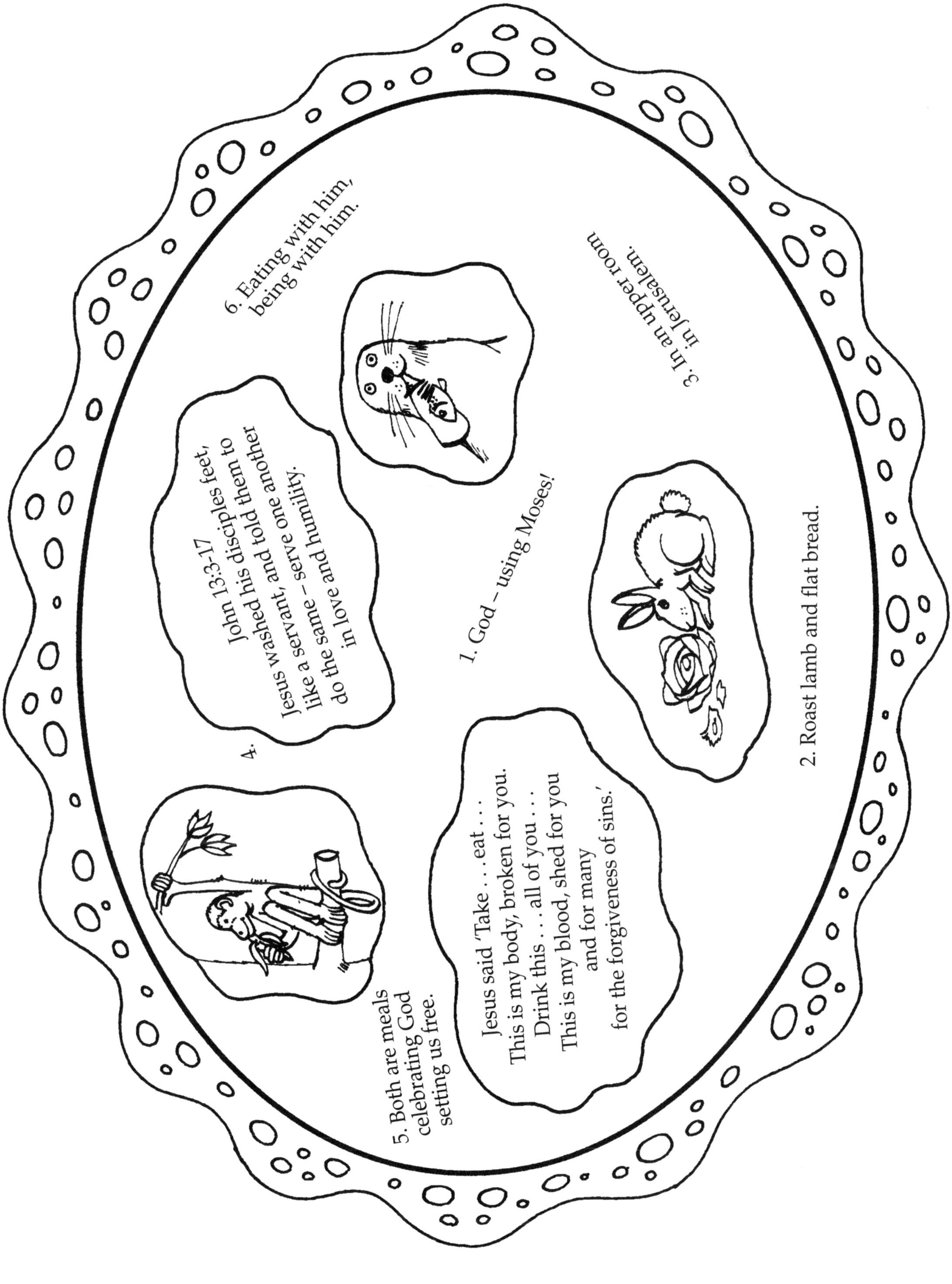

Pasta ecclesia (serves 8)

You will need:
2 lb (900 g) pasta (spaghetti, noodles, etc.)
2 large onions, chopped
2 cloves garlic, crushed
1 green pepper, deseeded and diced
1 yellow pepper, deseeded and diced
4 courgettes, sliced
4 carrots, chopped
4 oz (100 g) mushrooms, sliced
1 large aubergine, diced
1 lb (450 g) tomatoes, peeled and chopped
1 large can of chopped tomatoes
2 tablespoons chopped basil
salt and pepper to taste
2 tablespoons chopped parsley
some grated Parmesan cheese

What you do

Put all the ingredients except the pasta, parsley and cheese in a wok or large saucepan and add just enough water to cover the vegetables. Cook gently until the vegetables are tender, the water has mostly evaporated and the juices are thickened. (This will take 25-30 minutes.) Whenever you stir the vegetables, thank God for their different colours, shapes and textures. Give thanks, too, for the richness of different characters, looks and gifts of those in your church, and for all those who have grown, packed, delivered and sold the vegetables to you.

At the same time cook the pasta in plenty of salted boiling water until it is tender. (This will take about 15 minutes, but follow the instructions on the packet.) Drain the pasta, arrange it in a ring on a warm serving dish, and sprinkle with parsley. Taste and season the vegetable sauce and place in the centre of the pasta, sprinkled with grated cheese and a sprig of parsley. As you do this, pray for those who are going to eat it, that they may be fed not only with the food, but also nourished by God's love and blessing in their lives.

Pizza companiere (serves 8)

You will need:
For the pizza base:
1 lb (450 g) strong plain flour
2 teaspoons salt
2 teaspoons dried yeast
Half a pint (300 ml) lukewarm water

For the topping:
2 x 14 oz (397 g) cans chopped tomatoes
2 large onions, chopped
2 tablespoons olive oil
2 cloves garlic, crushed
salt and black pepper
8 oz (200 g) mozzarella cheese, sliced
8 oz (200 g) pepperoni, sliced
some olives and sliced red and green pepper to garnish

What you do

For the pizza base
Put the flour, yeast and salt in a bowl and add the warm water. Mix to a stiff dough and knead on a floured surface for 10 minutes. As you knead, think of God working his love into your church community, especially into any areas which are causing difficulty at the moment. Then put the dough into a warm, oiled bowl, oil the top and cover with clingfilm and leave in a warm place until it has doubled in size. As you do this, commend all the church community, its strengths and weaknesses, its joys and sorrows into God's loving keeping.

Knead the dough for another few minutes and press it into one huge (18 in/46 cm) or two smaller-sized (9 in/23 cm) pizza bases, on greased baking trays. Spoon over them the topping mixture and other ingredients and leave for 15 minutes in a warm place before baking in a hot oven (gas mark 7/220°C) for 20-30 minutes.

For the topping
Heat the oil in a large saucepan and add the onion and garlic. Fry gently until soft, then add the tomatoes and seasoning. Continue to cook until you have a sauce thick enough to spoon on the pizza base. Put this on the base first, then the cheese slices, then the pepperoni, olives and peppers. As you add all these thank God for the way we can enjoy all these different flavours together, and thank God, too, for the way he can use and enjoy all our different personalities, strengths and weaknesses in his church.

Next, please . . .

Two members of the Church Council are seated at a table, with notes and a pinger bell in front of them.

Arthur Grand Well, if she doesn't arrive in the next two minutes we start without her. I have better things to do with my evening than sit here with a gale blowing down my neck.

Kevin Clark Oh, are you in a draught under that broken window, Arthur? I could try blocking it a bit with one of the hymn boards, if you like.

Arthur Grand (*irritably*) No, no, sit down for heaven's sake. The numbers will all fall off and we'll end up singing 'Morning has broken' at Evensong. Where *is* that woman?

Vicar (*walking quietly in behind Arthur*) Right here!

Arthur Grand (*jumps in surprise*) Oh my goodness, Vicar. I do wish you'd get some louder shoes . . . and a watch, perhaps?

Vicar (*smiles brightly*) Yes, I'm sorry I'm late. Just as I was leaving the vicarage there was another bomb alert in the front garden, and a potential suicide phone call.

Arthur Grand Mmm, nothing really urgent then. Can we make a start, now the vicar's arrived?

Vicar Yes, let's begin right away. (*pings bell*) First applicant, please.

(*A very elderly person staggers on with a stick, and stands in front of the table.*)

Mrs Bloom Good evening, I'm Mrs Bloom. (*she coughs*) Excuse me – (*coughs*) oh dear me . . . (*She carries on coughing from time to time.*)

Kevin Clark She's a bit too old, isn't she? I mean . . . well, she's *very* old.

Arthur Grand Mmm. Don't know that age is supposed to matter that much, is it? Let's just look at the guidelines . . . (*They all shuffle through their notes.*)

Vicar No, apparently age isn't important.

Kevin Clark She isn't too healthy, either. What about that?

Arthur Grand No, it seems that health doesn't matter, so I suppose she's in.

Vicar Well, Mrs Bloom, thank you for coming. Perhaps you'd like to sit down over there for a minute. There's a few hymn books for you to read while you're waiting.

Mrs Bloom Oh, all right, dear, thank you. (*coughs*) Hope I brought my reading glasses – er, you don't have a large-print version, do you?

Arthur Grand I *knew* she'd be difficult!

Kevin Clark No, Mrs Bloom, but I can put it on the overhead projector, if you like – 'Abide with me', is it, or 'The Lord's my shepherd'? I've got both. (*He sets it up for her.*)

Mrs Bloom 'Abide with me' would be lovely. Thank you, young man. Very thoughtful . . . (*coughs*) Glad I came . . .

Vicar And here's some water, Mrs Bloom, for that cough.

Mrs Bloom Ah, thank you, dear. Very kind.

Vicar (*pings bell*) Next, please!

(*A young child walks on and stands at the table.*)

Harry Hello, I'm Harry.

Kevin Clark I'll just check his head for any lightning scars . . . no, he's not *that* Harry.

Arthur Grand He's a bit young though, isn't he? We don't include them this young, do we?

Vicar Actually, we're supposed to learn from this kind, I think you'll find.

Arthur Grand Mmm. This is going to be disruptive . . . I can feel it in my bones.

Kevin Clark I could give you a few old ASBs to sit on?

Arthur Grand You see – even *he* can't understand abstract ideas – how on earth are this sort (*pointing to Harry*) going to cope?

Vicar Perhaps we're the ones who are going to have to cope, Arthur. Anyway, Harry seems to fall in with the guidelines, so he's in. Would you like to sit over there with Mrs Bloom, Harry?

(*Harry goes to the chair by Mrs Bloom and starts showing her a toy from his pocket. They are obviously getting on well together.*)

Vicar Next, please!

(*A young person comes in, well pierced, and stands in front of the table.*)

Sasha Hi, I'm Sasha.

Kevin Clark We can't have people like this, can we?

Vicar Why not?

Kevin Clark Well . . . you know . . . not much like us, is it? And which is it, anyway? I know you're supposed to look at the shoes, but I've done that and I'm still undecided.

Arthur Grand You could phone a friend . . . oh no, he'd have to *have* a friend for that . . . OK, Kevin, I'm only joking.

Vicar The guidelines don't say anything about appearance being prohibitive. Rather the opposite, in fact.

Kevin Clark Are you . . . er . . . you *are* a human being, are you?

Sasha I was last time I looked.

Vicar Well, that settles it then. Human beings are in. Sasha's in. This has been quite a steep learning curve for us, I suspect.

Arthur Grand Mrs Bloom and Harry . . . er, sorry to interrupt your game . . . (*shouts*) Mrs Bloom and Harry, would you like to come over and meet Sasha?

(*They walk over to the table.*)

Vicar Yes, welcome to St Gumbo's church. It seems you are *all* most welcome. Indeed, even we ourselves are welcome –

All Everyone is welcome!

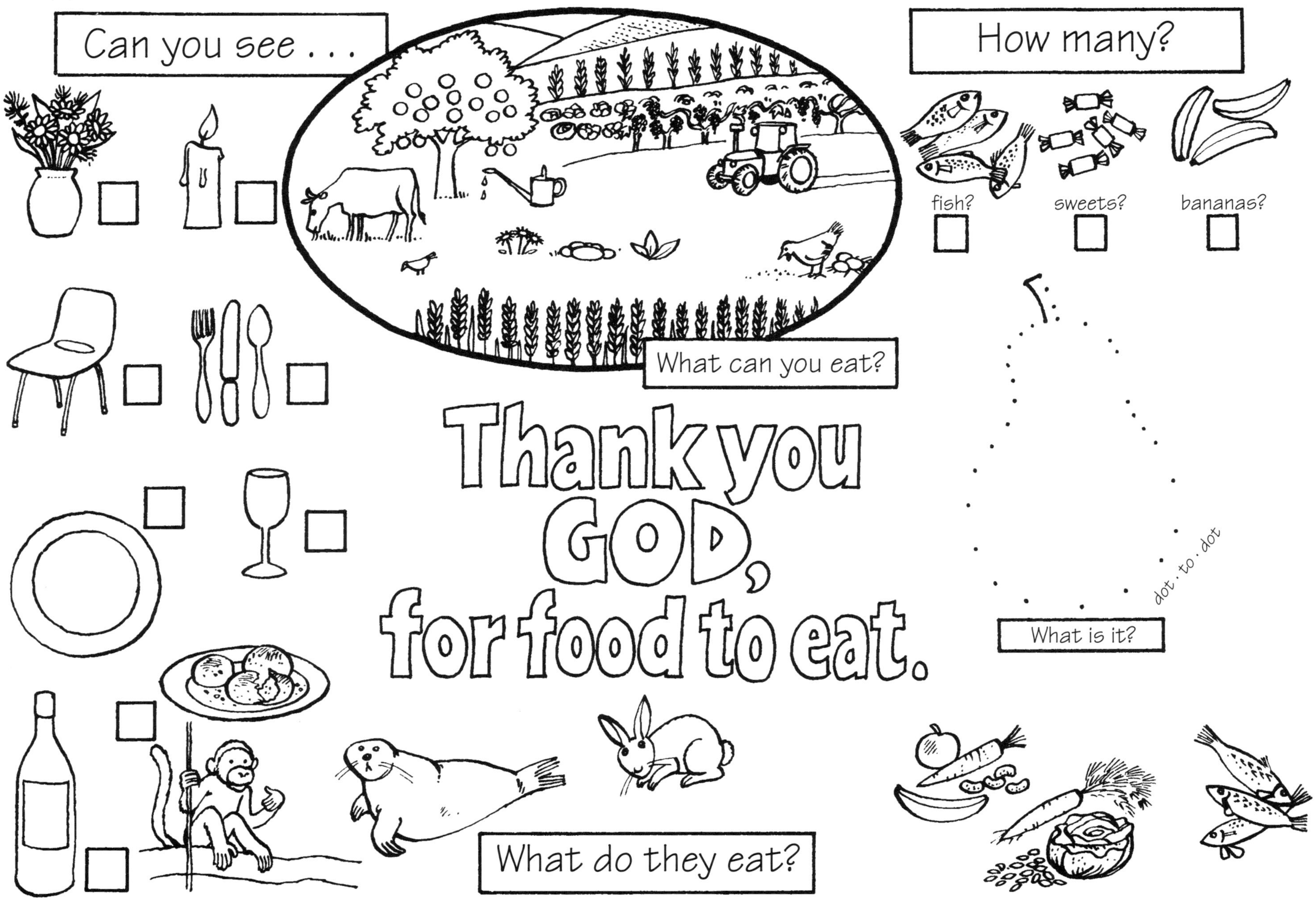
Can you see . . .
What can you eat?
How many?
fish?
sweets?
bananas?
dot . to . dot
What is it?
Thank you GOD, for food to eat.
What do they eat?

FACT FILE

Draw the person sitting facing you.

How many of us are here?

Shout this out when you hear the question.

How many people here do you know by name?

How old is the youngest person?

Draw the pot of flowers on your table.

What is the name of your church?

Draw you doing something you really enjoy.

THE PASSOVER

was the last MEAL eaten by the PEOPLE of ISRAEL when they were SLAVES in EGYPT. They ate it just BEFORE GOD led them OUT to FREEDOM, using MOSES.

P	E	O	P	L	E	H	C	U	S
O	A	A	D	M	O	S	E	S	L
U	M	S	K	B	G	V	J	T	A
T	G	I	S	R	A	E	L	F	V
B	N	O	K	O	T	F	S	R	E
B	E	E	D	P	V	M	I	E	S
H	J	F	Y	W	E	E	R	E	Z
O	C	G	O	D	Q	A	R	D	A
G	E	P	L	R	X	L	Y	O	L
L	A	S	T	F	E	I	N	M	Q

Blessed are you, Lord God of all creation.
Of your goodness we have this food to enjoy,
which earth has given
and human hands have made.

Blessed be GOD forever. Amen.

DID YOU KNOW . . . ?

The Passover is still eaten every year by Jewish people to remember God's love in rescuing them from slavery.

? ? ? ?

What do we call the Passover meal Jesus ate with his disciples just before he was killed?

What did Jesus say at that meal?

HINT: EAT UP ALL THE VEGETABLES!

QUIZ

1. What does the person on your left eat for breakfast? ☐
2. Can the person facing you:
   (a) wiggle their ears ☐
   (b) whistle ☐
   (c) cook ☐
3. How does the person next-but-one on your right prefer to eat an egg:
   (a) soft boiled ☐
   (b) hard boiled ☐
   (c) scrambled ☐
   (d) not if they can help it ☐
4. How many people at your table were born in this town? ☐
5. Who on your table has seen most of the world? ☐

Leader:	What have we been doing here?
You:	We've been eating and drinking together and getting to know one another better.
Leader:	How many of us are here?
Rocks:	☐
Women:	It's been much more than a meal. All this sharing makes us into a real community.
Men:	Like one big extended family.
Everyone:	The family of God, gathered to share food and friendship in God's company.
You:	It's a bit like the Passover meal.
Women:	What's the Passover?
Rocks:	The Passover was the last meal eaten by the people of Israel when they were slaves in Egypt. They ate it just before God let them out to freedom, using Moses.
You:	And Jesus ate the Passover with his friends on the night before he died.
Men:	What do we call that meal?
Rocks:	The Last Supper.
Everyone:	Whenever we come to Communion we gather as the family of God with Jesus present among us.
Leader:	Let us go in God's peace.
Everyone:	Thanks be to God.

WELCOME!

We do hope you enjoy the meal

On my right is

On my left is

Facing me is

Cartoon pics of these people

THE POSTSCRIPT

Leader:	What have we been doing here?
Boulders:	We've been eating and drinking together and getting to know one another better.
Leader:	How many of us are here?
Rocks:	☐ (Encourage them to shout their answer)
Women:	It's been much more than a meal. All this sharing makes us into a real community.
Men:	Like one big extended family.
Everyone:	The family of God, gathered to share food and friendship in God's company.
Boulders:	It's a bit like the Passover meal.
Women:	What's the Passover?
Rocks:	The Passover was the last meal eaten by the people of Israel when they were slaves in Egypt. They ate it just before God let them out to freedom, using Moses.
Boulders:	And Jesus ate the Passover with his friends on the night before he died.
Men:	What do we call that meal?
Rocks:	The Last Supper.
Everyone:	Whenever we come to Communion we gather as the family of God with Jesus present among us.
Leader:	Let us go in God's peace.
Everyone:	Thanks be to God!

We all join in the Grace

Blessed are you,
Lord God of all creation.
Of your goodness we have this food to enjoy,
which earth has given and human hands
have made.

Blessed be God for ever.
Amen

before our meal.

Colour the mosaic to look like a picture of NEW LIFE.

QUIZ NIGHT

1. Who led the people of Israel out of slavery in Egypt?
2. What did they eat the night before they went?
3. Where did Jesus eat the Last Supper?
4. What did Jesus teach the disciples by washing their feet?
5. How is our Communion Service like a Passover?
6. How did Jesus' friends recognise him after he had risen from the dead?

Clue: Eat the vegetables!

A Passover Celebration

Introduction

Our understanding of the Eucharist is greatly helped if we can share regularly the uplifting experience of a Passover meal. Familiar signs and symbols take on new depths of meaning, and the Last Supper is seen in the context of God's saving love stretching from creation over the whole course of human history. As Christians we share common roots with our Jewish brothers and sisters, and the festival of Passover is part of our shared faith heritage. So to celebrate the meal like this together is a wonderful opportunity to discover a fresh way of telling the story of God's love, and finding it to be our own story.

The traditional order, or Seder, of this special evening takes place in the home, by candlelight, with family and friends around the table. It tells the profound story of the people's slavery in Egypt and their God rescuing them. The story is told through tastes and textures, prayers, readings and songs, the drinking of four cups of wine/grape juice, the breaking of bread, the eating of specially prepared food, and, through questions asked by the children, about what the meal means. The occasion is full of thanksgiving and praise as we remember God's love and care, but also full of empathy with the suffering of all who are oppressed and in great need. Rather than being simply a festive meal built on memories, the experience brings those saving events right into the present, binding the community together as children of God, reliving their escape in the presence of their Creator and Redeemer.

So both Jews and Christians meet with God in the simple act of sharing a cup of wine and a piece of bread together, full of thankfulness and praise for the One who made us, provides for us, and rescues us. And of course it was during a Seder meal that Jesus spoke of his own life being broken and poured out to save us from the slavery of sin. The bittersweet tastes of the Passover are there too in our Eucharist, as we thank God for saving us, yet know it to be through Jesus' costly suffering. We rejoice in the way we have been set free, yet at the same time hunger for the whole world to know that freedom.

Preparations for Passover

Have a good clear-out of the church hall before the meal, paying particular attention to anything which has been sitting there for ages without being used. Traditionally this is the perfect time to distribute things we are no longer using to those who can make use of them!

Set the tables beautifully, with cloths and, if possible, real cutlery, glasses and dishes, rather than disposable ones. Each place setting will also need a fingerbowl with water in it. Involve the children in preparing the place names and place mats (see pages 187-190), and arrange the table so that everyone can see the leader's section, which should feel central, rather than separate.

The buffet meal and all the special dishes are arranged in clusters on each stretch of table, so that everyone has access to the same kind of food. Wine and grape juice are placed at regular intervals around the table and one place is left empty.

For each group of six people you will need the following:

- candles and flowers
- a glass of salty water
- sprigs of parsley or another springtime herb
- dish of maror ('bitter herb' of slavery, such as horseradish sauce)
- dish of haroseth ('sweetness of freedom', a mixture of chopped or grated apples, raisins, finely chopped nuts and cinnamon, made into little balls with grapejuice or wine and coated with chopped nuts; or you can use dates)
- a basket of matzo (unleavened bread)

At the leader's table you will need the following:

- a candlestick for at least two candles, and some matches
- a glass of salty water
- a beautiful plate containing the springtime herbs, the bitter herb (maror), the sweet stuff (haroseth), a lamb or chicken bone and a hard-boiled egg
- three squares of matzo (unleavened bread) under a napkin

The rest of the food for the buffet can be anything delicious, and it is served with the matzo, the haroseth and vegetables.

*The order of service**

1. The candle lighting

The leader welcomes everyone to the Passover, which is a celebration of the way God rescues his people from slavery. Everyone is asked to keep silence as they get ready to receive God's blessing at this Passover meal.

A short time of silence

The leader lights the candles, saying:

Blessed are you, Lord God of all creation.
Of your goodness we have the gift of light to lighten our darkness.

The light is passed all around the tables until every candle in the room is lit. ('The Lord is my light' (Taizé) may be sung quietly.) As this is happening the leader prays:

May the brightness of these small lights
remind us of the great light of your love
which brings us joy and hope.
Blessed be God for ever!

2. We say Grace

We fill our glasses and raise them as we pray:

Blessed are you, Lord God of all creation.
Through your goodness we have this wine to drink,
fruit of the vine and work of human hands.
Blessed be God for ever!

Everyone drinks their wine or grape juice and fills the glass again.

3. We wash our hands

As we wash our fingers in the bowl of water we pray:

Blessed are you, Lord God of all creation.
You alone can make us clean.
You alone can make us holy.
Blessed be God for ever!

(At the Last Supper it was not just hands that were washed, but feet as well.)

4. Eating a springtime herb

The leader dips some of the parsley into the salty water, saying:

Blessed are you, Lord God of all creation.
Each springtime, through your goodness,
the earth brings forth plants and fruit,
to renew the world we inhabit.
Blessed be God for ever!

Everyone dips some parsley in salty water and eats it.

5. The bread-sharing

The leader picks up the three pieces of matzo, and puts aside half a piece for unexpected guests, saying:

Blessed are you, Lord God of all creation.
Through your goodness we have this bread to eat
which earth has given and human hands have made.
Let us always share our bread with the hungry.

*An A5 eight-page photocopiable version can be found on pages 201-204

We remember now all those who are persecuted or poor.
Next year may we and they be free.
Our Passover cannot be complete until all God's people are free.
Blessed be God for ever!

This is the bread of pain and affliction
which our ancestors ate in Egypt, when they were slaves,
and which our oppressed brothers and sisters eat now.
Take this, all of you, and eat it.

The leader shares the bread with those around, and everyone else shares the bread near them with one another, dipping it in the salty water of tears, remembering the poor and oppressed. The piece of bread put aside is now hidden, for the children to find later on.

Leader:

Let one of the children open our door
to show that we welcome all who are hungry,
in body and in spirit.

One of the children opens the door wide.

All:

Let all who hunger for bread and for freedom,
for truth, and for inner peace,
come and share the bread which our God provides for us.

6. The story

The children:

Why is this night different from all other nights?

Leader:

Thank you for asking that question, children. It is always good to ask questions, and find out the answers. That way you will learn the story we share and understand the traditions we value.

Tonight is different from all other nights because we are celebrating something amazing. Once our ancestors were slaves of Pharaoh in Egypt, and God rescued our people, bringing us out of slavery into the promise of freedom and redemption. Our terrible suffering was turned into a time of happiness and blessing.

Child:

Why do we eat only flat bread without yeast tonight?

When Pharaoh let the people go they had to escape in a great hurry. They had no time to wait for their bread to rise, so they baked it flat, like the bread we are eating tonight.

Child:

Why do we eat bitter herbs tonight?

The bitter herbs remind us that life was bitter and sad for the people when they were oppressed as slaves in the land of Egypt. When we taste the bitter herbs we taste the bitterness of every person who is sad and oppressed, and longs to be free.

Child:

Why do we have the sweet stuff to eat?

The sweet stuff reminds us of the sweetness of freedom when God brought us out of slavery. It reminds us of the sweetness of God's goodness and love which always triumphs over evil.

Child:

Why do we eat parsley?

We have parsley because it reminds us of all the fresh green plants of springtime which bring fresh new life to the world each year. Our God loves us and looks after us, and that makes us happy.

Child:

Why do we dip our parsley and bread in salt water?

The salt water reminds us of tears which people cry when they are very sad. As we taste the salty water we remember the tears of the people when they were slaves, and the tears of everyone who is not free or at peace with God.

Child:

Why is there a lamb bone?

Because the people ate a lamb that last night in Egypt, just before they were rescued. They put its blood on their doorposts and so they were protected from the plague of death that night. This was the tenth and last plague before Pharaoh agreed to let Moses and the people go. Let us express our compassion for the Egyptians who suffered those plagues. They were our enemies, but still they were children of God and fellow human beings, and we feel sorry for all who suffer – whether they are friends or enemies.

As each plague is mentioned, everyone dips a finger in their wine and drips it on their plate to remember the suffering:

Blood . . . Frogs . . . Vermin . . . Flies . . . Cattle disease . . . Boils . . . Hailstones . . . Locusts . . . Darkness . . . Death of every firstborn.

Child:

Why are we taking so much trouble over this meal tonight – with clean cloths and candles and flowers and party food?

Because thanks to God's loving rescue, we have all been set free from slavery and sin! In spite of all the tears and sadness in our world there is lots and lots to thank God for, and we want to enjoy thanking him as well as we can for all he has done in our lives.

Blessed be God for ever!

Everyone drinks their wine or grape juice, and refills the glass.

Leader:

Now we are ready to enjoy the Passover meal!

All:

We'll taste the bitterness of pain and oppression
and the sweetness of hope and freedom.
We'll eat thankfully of all God's gifts
and rejoice that we can share this time
and this food together in God's company.

7. The meal

The meal is eaten.

8. Hide and seek

After the meal the children can search for the afikomen (the hidden piece of matzo) and the one who finds it is given a reward. This piece of bread is broken and shared out among everyone. The bread is held as the leader says:

This bread is broken and shared to remind us of the Passover lambs which were sacrificed and shared, to give the people strength for their journey ahead and protection from the plague of death.

Everyone eats the fragment of bread.

A song is sung, such as 'Our God is so great, so strong and so mighty', 'You shall go out with joy', 'Give me joy in my heart' or 'Jubilate everybody'.

9. Grace after the meal

Leader:

The Bible tells us that when you have eaten and are satisfied you shall thank the Lord our God for the good land which he has given you. We have eaten and are satisfied, so let us thank God now.

Everyone raises their glasses as they pray:

All:

O Lord our God, we praise you
and thank you for feeding us all in body and spirit.

Women and girls:

We thank you for the good earth
and its fruitfulness;

Men and boys:

We thank you for the friendship we have shared tonight
and for the loving kindness you shower on us each day.

All:

We thank you for freeing us from slavery and sin
through the gift of your forgiveness.
We pray that all God's children may be freed
from hatred and hunger, oppression and guilt,
free to live contentedly in your love. Amen.

Everyone drinks their wine or grape juice

Leader:

Let us go in God's peace.
Peace for us and peace for all people in the world.
No more war. No more oppression.
Justice and peace for everyone.
Let it be so. **Amen. Let it be so.**

Everyone sings 'Shalom, my friends' (Billington)

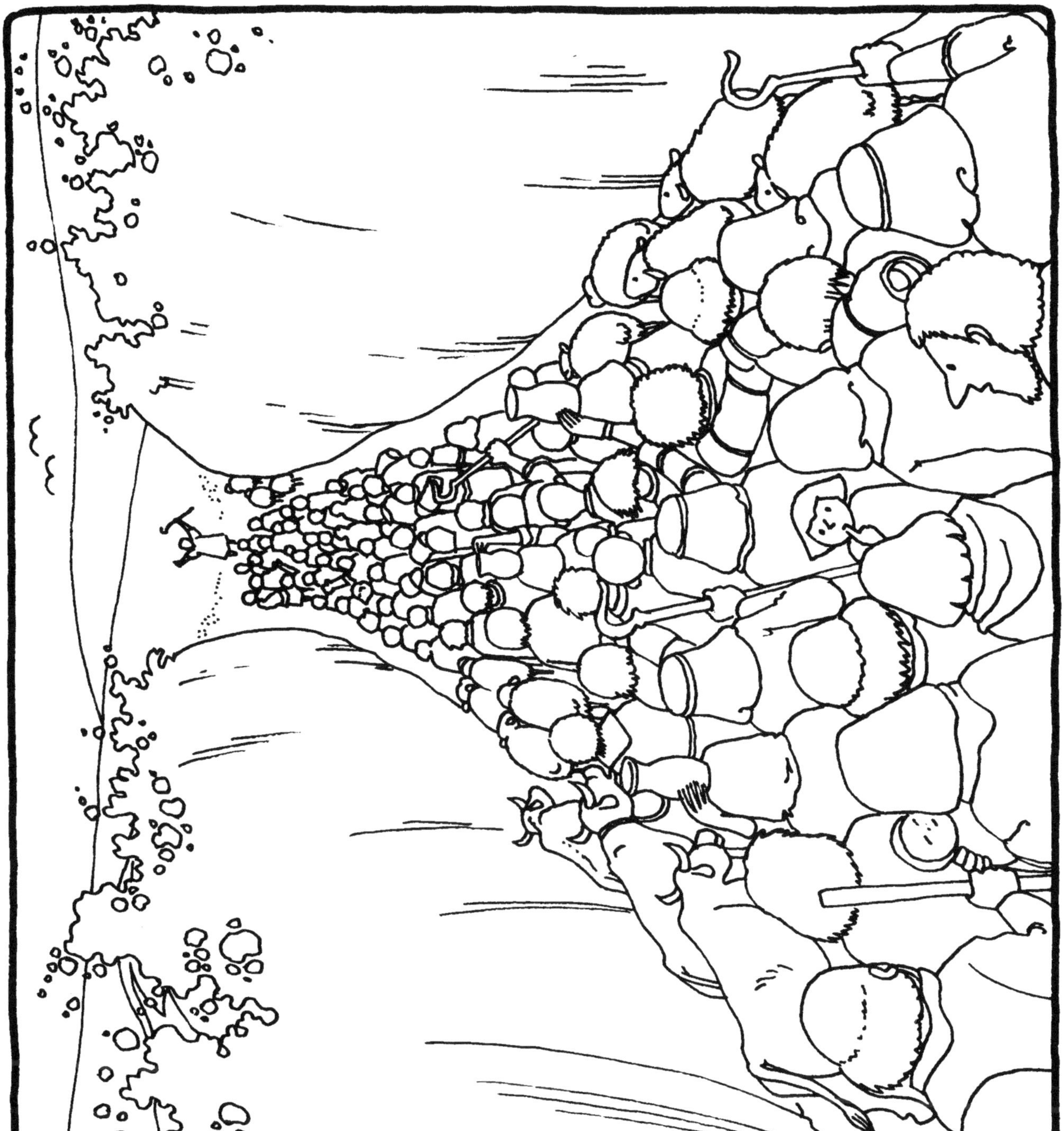

Can you spot . . .

The people of Israel were slaves.
It was a hard life.
Please rescue us !!!
The people cried out to God,
'Please come and rescue us!'
Then Moses was born.
He was put in a basket.
Pharaoh's daughter found him and
brought him up as a Prince of Egypt.
Draw flames on the bush.
God spoke to Moses from a burning bush.
'I will lead my people to freedom,' God said.
Draw Pharaoh on his throne.
Moses went to Pharaoh. 'Let my
people go,' he said. 'No,' said Pharaoh.
Draw one of the plagues.
At last . . . 'OK, you can go!'
God sent terrible plagues – water into blood,
frogs, gnats, flies, livestock disease, boils, thunder
and hail, locusts, darkness, death of the firstborn.
Draw the blood marking the doorposts.
The people ate their last supper in Egypt
dressed ready to go. This was the Passover meal.
. . . and God led his people out to freedom.

BOTH PASSOVER AND COMMUNION
(Colour orange)
ONLY COMMUNION
(Colour yellow)
SACRIFICE
FORGIVENESS
LIBERATION
CHURCH
THANKSGIVING
RED SEA
LEAVING BEHIND
PRAYER
TOKEN MEAL
ONLY PASSOVER
(Colour red)
COMPLETE MEAL
SCRIPTURE READING
MOVING FORWARD
WINE
COMMUNITY MEMORY
BREAD
FREEDOM
REMEMBERING PAIN

making
CONNECTIONS
Think of the Passover
Why was the Passover a 'Last Supper'.
What animal's blood saved the people at Passover?
What kind of setting free?
Think of the Last Supper
Why was the Last Supper a 'Passover'.
Any connections?
What kind of setting free?

The Emmaus Meal

Introduction

It was as two disciples of Jesus walked miserably home to Emmaus from Jerusalem on the Sunday after the crucifixion that they were joined by a stranger. He walked with them, meeting them where they were in their thinking and leading them to understand God's unfolding rescue plan. And it was when the stranger broke bread that they suddenly recognised him as the risen Jesus. The encounter changed the direction of their lives, sending them immediately straight back to Jerusalem, and, in the longer term, out into the world to spread the Good News and live the risen life.

Our Emmaus meal picks up on the way Jesus meets us where we are, rather than where we think we ought to be, journeys with us making sense of what we don't understand, and reveals himself to us in the breaking of bread.

Everyone meets first at the church, homing in on the sadness of the disciples after the crucifixion and before their knowledge of resurrection. Everyone then sets off in groups of five or six, following clues along the way which lead them both to tracing the fulfilment of prophecies and to someone's home, where soup is served in cups, and each group is given a small loaf to break and share. The pace and mood changes and the groups walk back to the church, where there is rejoicing and sharing of discoveries in the context of worship, and a buffet meal is served.

This meal is a discipleship journey.

The starting point

Everyone meets in church, where a large wooden cross is standing with a label hung on it which reads, 'So where do we go from here?'

If the church has Stations of the Cross, use these pictures; otherwise stick some pictures of the Passion or of the Via Dolorosa in Jerusalem around the walls. Begin the worship by inviting everyone in their own time to walk around the pictures or stations in silence, while recorded music is played (such as Bach's *St Matthew Passion*, the soundtrack music from *Schindler's List* or *Gladiator*, or anything else which expresses pain and suffering).

Sing together one of the Passion hymns, such as 'Were you there when they crucified my Lord'? (omitting the final verse at the moment) or 'O sacred head, sore wounded'. The mood is reflective and solemn as people join the disciples in their confusion, shock and grief.

Reading – Luke 24:13-24.

Now the people are sent out, group by group, with their first clue. This is a staggered start, and they will be going at different speeds, so the soup and bread people shouldn't have to cope with feeding everyone at the same moment.

The journey of discovery

Four stewards are posted at certain points on the route, ready to give out jigsaw pieces (see page 193) and the next clue. All the clues help the group make sense of the seeming failure of the crucifixion, and the identity and mission of Jesus. The clues are coded (see page 194) and each group is provided with a decoder (see page 193) so they can crack the codes and read the message.

Clue 1 (given out to each group in church)

(a) Coded directions to the place of the next clue

(b) Coded message to think about: If Jesus really was the Messiah, why did he end up being crucified to death?

(c) Luke 24:25-27

Clue 2 (given out at the first checkpoint)

(a) Coded directions to the next checkpoint

(b) Numbers 14:11; 2 Samuel 7:16 (spoken by the prophet Nathan to King David); Jonah 1:17; Zephaniah 3:16-18; Isaiah 53:4-12

(c) A section of the picture

Clue 3 (given out at the second checkpoint)

(a) Coded directions to the next checkpoint

(b) Question to think about on the way: What kind of a kingdom was Jesus bringing in by such a death?

(c) A section of the picture

Clue 4 (given out at the third checkpoint)

(a) Coded directions to the home where soup and bread will be served

(b) Jeremiah 31:33-34; John 15:12-14; Mark 10:42-45; Luke 22:19. Compare these references with your own ideas.

(c) A section of the picture

Clue 5 (given out with the bread at the house)

(a) Read this while one of the group breaks the bread and shares it out: Luke 24:28-32.

(b) A section of the picture (given after the eating of soup and bread)

(c) Coded instruction (to be decoded when you receive the jigsaw piece): Without a moment's delay they set out and returned to Jerusalem.

Meanwhile, back at Jerusalem . . .

Candles and flowers have been placed all around the cross, and the label replaced with a new one: 'It's true! He's alive! He walks with us and breaks bread with us!' Worship music is playing and the mood is festive and joyful.

As people make their way back they are each given a lighted candle, so that as the church fills with people it fills with light. They join in with the on-going worship until everyone has arrived. Someone from each group brings the jigsaw pieces of the picture and works on the floor to piece it together. When complete it reads: 'As the Father has sent me, so I am sending you.' All lights are now switched on.

Reading – Luke 24:32-49

A rousing resurrection hymn is sung, such as 'Thine be the glory', 'Love's redeeming work is done', or 'Alleluia, sing to Jesus'.

A buffet is served in the church or hall – preferably including fish!

The code breaker

1. Cut out both circles and stick on thin card.
2. Join the smaller circle on to the larger using a split pin.

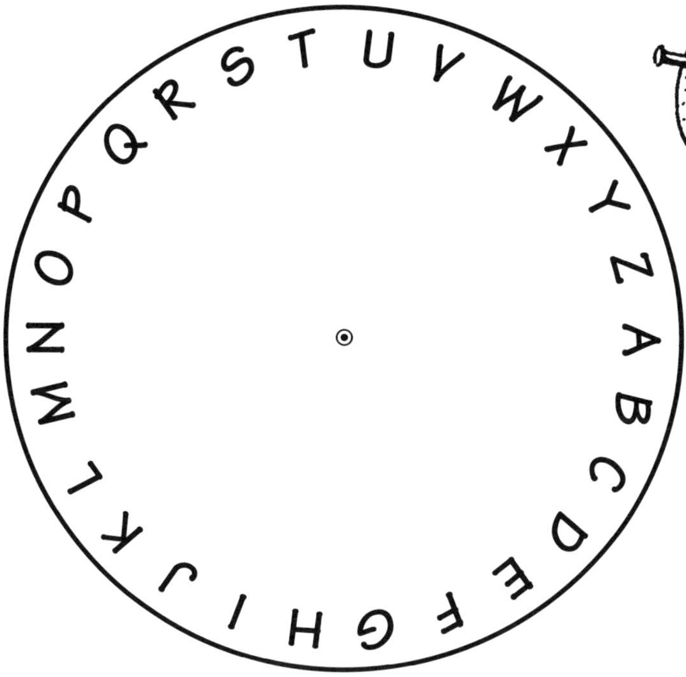

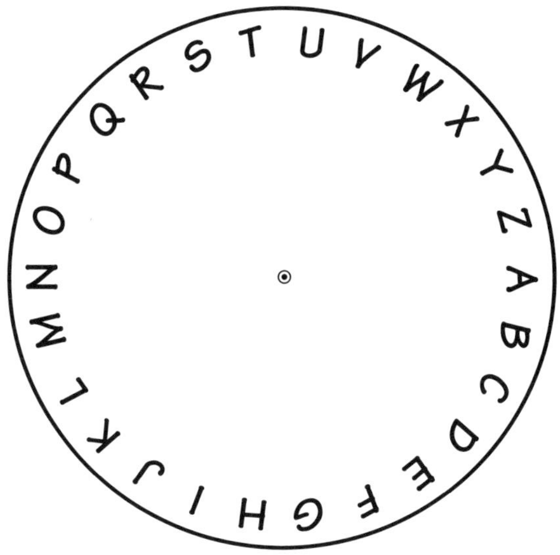

The jigsaw picture

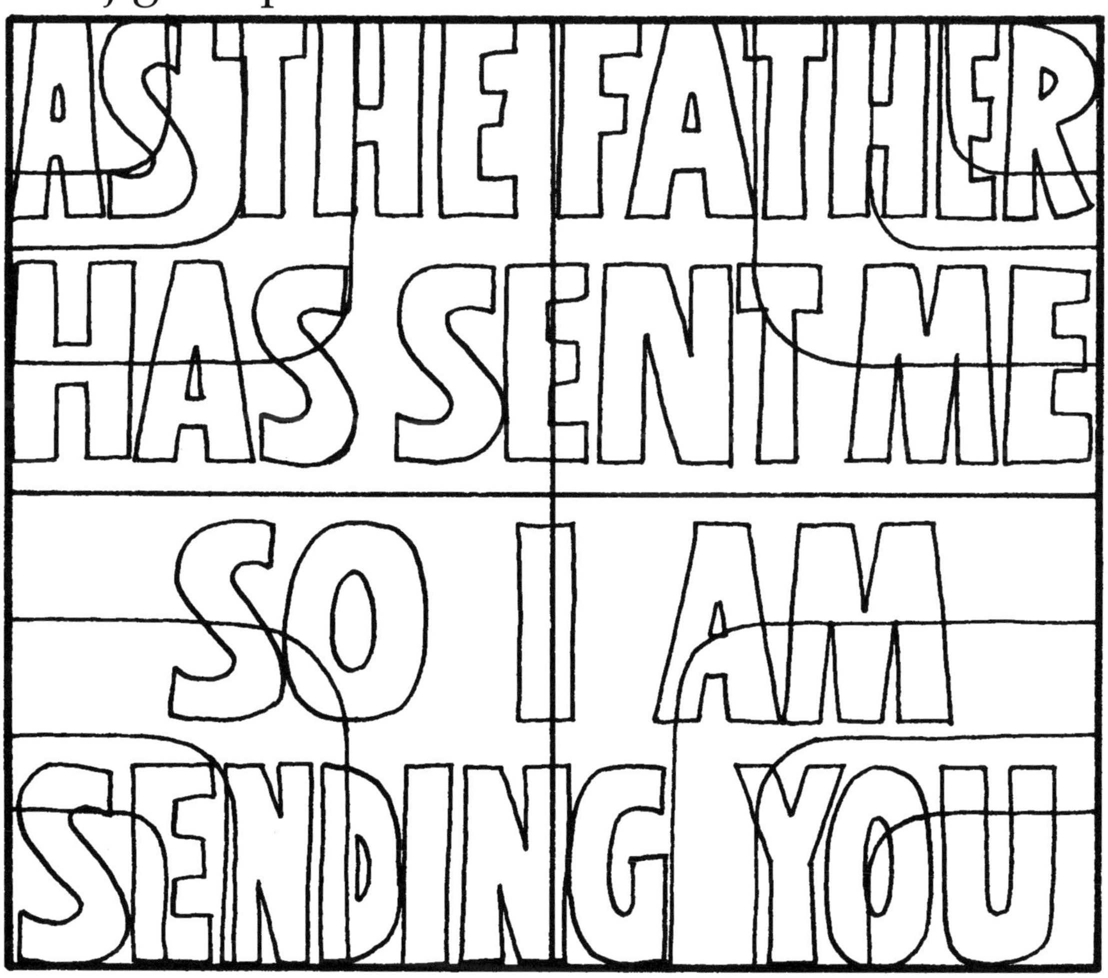

Make this as large as possible and cut it into enough pieces for each group to have four sections. Larger gatherings will need smaller pieces.

Enlarge, copy and colour.

Coded messages

Clue 1
Match the A to the T

(b) Coded message reads: PM QLZBZ YLHSSF DHZ AOL TLZZPHO, DOF KPK OL LUK BW ILPUN JYBJPMPLK AV KLHAO?

Clue 2
Match the G to the T

Clue 3
Match the M to the T

Clue 4
Match the J to the T

Clue 5
Match the Q to the T

(c) Coded message reads: TFQELRQ X JLJBKQ'P ABIXV QEBV PBQ LRQ XKA OBQROKBA QL GBORPXIBJ.

APPENDIX

Rejoice in the Lord always

To be played as a round with the second instrument entering at B

Music: Evelyn Tarner, arr. Christopher Tambling

Rejoice in the Lord always

Two-note part

Open-string part

The Ash Grove

Music: traditional Welsh melody, arr. Noel Rawsthorne

Bm(D)
A
E(-)
A
D
Bm(D)
Em
A7
D
G
A7
D

The Ash Grove

Two-note part

Open-string part

Men and boys:

We thank you for the friendship we have shared tonight
and for the loving kindness you shower on us each day.

All:

We thank you for freeing us from slavery and sin
through the gift of your forgiveness.
We pray that all God's children may be freed
from hatred and hunger, oppression and guilt,
free to live contentedly in your love. Amen.

Everyone drinks their wine or grape juice

Leader:

Let us go in God's peace.
Peace for us and peace for all people in the world.
No more war. No more oppression.
Justice and peace for everyone.
Let it be so. **Amen. Let it be so.**

Everyone sings 'Shalom, my friends'

A Passover Celebration

Order of service

1. The candle lighting

The leader welcomes everyone to the Passover, which is a celebration of the way God rescues his people from slavery. Everyone is asked to keep silence as they get ready to receive God's blessing at this Passover meal.

A short time of silence

The leader lights the candles, saying:

Blessed are you, Lord God of all creation.
Of your goodness we have the gift of light
to lighten our darkness.

The light is passed all around the tables until every candle in the room is lit. ('The Lord is my light' may be sung quietly. As this is happening the leader prays:

May the brightness of these small lights
remind us of the great light of your love
which brings us joy and hope.
Blessed be God for ever!

2. We say Grace

We fill our glasses and raise them as we pray:

Blessed are you, Lord God of all creation.
Through your goodness we have this wine to drink,
fruit of the vine and work of human hands.
Blessed be God for ever!

Everyone drinks their wine or grape juice and fills the glass again.

3. We wash our hands

As we wash our fingers in the bowl of water we pray:

7. The meal

The meal is eaten.

8. Hide and seek

After the meal the children can search for the afikomen (the hidden piece of matzo) and the one who finds it is given a reward. This piece of bread is broken and shared out among everyone. The bread is held as the leader says:

This bread is broken and shared to remind us of the Passover lambs which were sacrificed and shared, to give the people strength for their journey ahead and protection from the plague of death.

Everyone eats the fragment of bread.

A song is sung, such as 'Our God is so great, so strong and so mighty', 'You shall go out with joy', 'Give me joy in my heart' or 'Jubilate everybody'.

9. Grace after the meal

Leader:

The Bible tells us that when you have eaten and are satisfied you shall thank the Lord our God for the good land which he has given you. We have eaten and are satisfied, so let us thank God now.

Everyone raises their glasses as they pray:

All:

O Lord our God, we praise you
and thank you for feeding us all in body and spirit.

Women and girls:

We thank you for the good earth
and its fruitfulness;

agreed to let Moses and the people go. Let us express our compassion for the Egyptians who suffered those plagues. They were our enemies, but still they were children of God and fellow human beings, and we feel sorry for all who suffer – whether they are friends or enemies.

As each plague is mentioned, everyone dips a finger in their wine and drips it on their plate to remember the suffering:

Blood . . . Frogs . . . Vermin . . . Flies . . . Cattle disease . . . Boils . . . Hailstones . . . Locusts . . . Darkness . . . Death of every firstborn.

Child:

Why are we taking so much trouble over this meal tonight – with clean cloths and candles and flowers and party food?

Because thanks to God's loving rescue, we have all been set free from slavery and sin! In spite of all the tears and sadness in our world there is lots and lots to thank God for, and we want to enjoy thanking him as well as we can for all he has done in our lives.

Blessed be God for ever!

Everyone drinks their wine or grape juice, and refills the glass.

Leader:

Now we are ready to enjoy the Passover meal!

All:

We'll taste the bitterness of pain and oppression
and the sweetness of hope and freedom.
We'll eat thankfully of all God's gifts
and rejoice that we can share this time
and this food together in God's company.

Blessed are you, Lord God of all creation.
You alone can make us clean.
You alone can make us holy.
Blessed be God for ever!

(At the Last Supper it was not just hands that were washed, but feet as well.)

4. Eating a springtime herb

The leader dips some of the parsley into the salty water, saying:

Blessed are you, Lord God of all creation.
Each springtime, through your goodness,
the earth brings forth plants and fruit,
to renew the world we inhabit.
Blessed be God for ever!

Everyone dips some parsley in salty water and eats it.

5. The bread-sharing

The leader picks up the three pieces of matzo, and puts aside half a piece for unexpected guests, saying:

Blessed are you, Lord God of all creation.
Through your goodness we have this bread to eat
which earth has given and human hands have made.
Let us always share our bread with the hungry.
We remember now all those who are persecuted or poor.
Next year may we and they be free.
Our Passover cannot be complete
until all God's people are free.
Blessed be God for ever!

This is the bread of pain and affliction
which our ancestors ate in Egypt, when they were slaves,
and which our oppressed brothers and sisters eat now.
Take this, all of you, and eat it.

The leader shares the bread with those around, and everyone else shares the bread near them with one another, dipping it in the salty water of tears, remembering the poor and oppressed. The piece of bread put aside is now hidden, for the children to find later on.

Leader:

Let one of the children open our door
to show that we welcome all who are hungry,
in body and in spirit.

One of the children opens the door wide.

All:

Let all who hunger for bread and for freedom,
for truth, and for inner peace,
come and share the bread which our God provides for us.

6. The story

The children:

Why is this night different from all other nights?

Leader:

Thank you for asking that question, children. It is always good to ask questions, and find out the answers. That way you will learn the story we share and understand the traditions we value.

Tonight is different from all other nights because we are celebrating something amazing. Once our ancestors were slaves of Pharaoh in Egypt, and God rescued our people, bringing us out of slavery into the promise of freedom and redemption. Our terrible suffering was turned into a time of happiness and blessing.

Child:

Why do we eat only flat bread without yeast tonight?

When Pharaoh let the people go they had to escape in a great hurry. They had no time to wait for their bread to rise, so they baked it flat, like the bread we are eating tonight.

Child:

Why do we eat bitter herbs tonight?

The bitter herbs remind us that life was bitter and sad for the people when they were oppressed as slaves in the land of Egypt. When we taste the bitter herbs we taste the bitterness of every person who is sad and oppressed, and longs to be free.

Child:

Why do we have the sweet stuff to eat?

The sweet stuff reminds us of the sweetness of freedom when God brought us out of slavery. It reminds us of the sweetness of God's goodness and love which always triumphs over evil.

Child:

Why do we eat parsley?

We have parsley because it reminds us of all the fresh green plants of springtime which bring fresh new life to the world each year. Our God loves us and looks after us, and that makes us happy.

Child:

Why do we dip our parsley and bread in salt water?

The salt water reminds us of tears which people cry when they are very sad. As we taste the salty water we remember the tears of the people when they were slaves, and the tears of everyone who is not free or at peace with God.

Child:

Why is there a lamb bone?

Because the people ate a lamb that last night in Egypt, just before they were rescued. They put its blood on their door-posts and so they were protected from the plague of death that night. This was the tenth and last plague before Pharaoh